Religious Newspapers
in the Old Northwest to 1861

WESLEY NORTON

Religious Newspapers in the Old Northwest to 1861: A History, Bibliography, and Record of Opinion

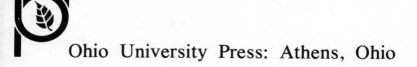 Ohio University Press: Athens, Ohio

To the memory of
HAZEL D. NORTON
and
KENNETH ALAN NORTON

TABLE OF CONTENTS

PREFACE

The immense energy and endurance of religion in America is quickly sensed when one enters the libraries of the numerous denominational colleges of antebellum origin in the states of the Old Northwest. The files of religious newspapers stored in those libraries attest also to the comprehensive sweep of religious interests and to the depth of religious commitment in that generation. The papers are the vibrant remains of the personalities and careers of the scores of men who, with an extravagant vision, became their editors and proprietors.

The newspaper was one of several agencies which religious societies developed to promote their multiple objectives. It was published weekly whenever possible to carry both the "good news" of the gospel and secular news and comment within a religious framework. The clergy who conducted them intended to save men and make for them, and fit them for, a kingdom which had both religious and secular dimensions. The combination of religious and secular function, unique to that generation, makes the religious newspaper the most revealing source of the complex motives, interests, and opinions of the religiously inclined. In reaching for their goal, the sponsors of this enterprise authentically reflected and influenced important segments of the public, with all classes of Americans being involved.

There is a particular value in a survey of this institution in the Old Northwest. The region was in many respects and in many areas a frontier, yet it blended all elements of the American population and of the American experience. Cincinnati, the principal publishing center in the region, as a thriving city of more than 160,000 in 1860, was but one of several flourishing urban areas. Even so, important denominational presses had been very recently turning out papers on farms and many were still operating in remote villages. Several denominations established their first publishing centers in the Northwest or had moved them there before 1860 and were sending papers back to their members in the East. The proponent of religion in the West was both proudly American and proudly aware of the impingement of the West upon American civilization. His multiplication of religious newspapers emphasizes that the growing edge of this and other religious enterprise was in his domain.

The assortment of religious papers in the Old Northwest demonstrates how real individualism and diversity were in the religious life of the region; so much so that personalities, ideas, and methods of the period must seem remote and uncongenial to the more ecumenical and cosmopolitan modern temper. It would, however, dishonor the personnel associated with this activity to treat them as merely quaint or to destroy their individuality by overzealous generalization. One of the great sources of pride among men of all faiths was their right and ability to be different. Certainly the truth of America's past cannot be known unless scholars are willing to experience the inconvenience of viewing candidly this extraordinary diversity as a daily fact of life. This perspective is vividly revealed in examination of the entire spectrum of Protestants, Catholics, and Jews publishing next door to one another, competing with one another, and uninhibitedly placing their respective views before the public.

The author's indebtedness is extensive. The personnel of more than two score libraries from Texas to New England gave their generous co-operation. The staff of the Lamar University library, especially Miss Maxine

Johnston, rendered very efficient service. Franklin and Marshal College, Catholic University of America, Hebrew Union College, and Concordia Seminary lent material, and the Presbyterian Historical Society arranged the filming of some key papers in their collections. Mrs. Amanda Langerno translated some Norwegian papers and Mrs. F. L. Braunfeld a German paper to which the author did not have access. The author is grateful to his colleagues, Professors Robert Olson, the late Earl Fornell, and Olga Harvill for having read and commented on portions of the manuscript. Members of the history department at Lamar University have been responsible for a congenial atmosphere in which to do the work of this profession. The Lamar Research Center assisted with the material support of many aspects of the research. The Penrose Fund of the American Philosophical Society provided the means for far-ranging travel during two consecutive summers. Both sources were indispensable to the completion of the project.

The major indebtedness of the author is to the members of his family. His parents, Leonard C. and the late Hazel D. Norton, helped provide the qualities involved in working on any long-range project. His wife, Lottie, furnished moral support and typed and retyped the manuscript even while busy with a professional life of her own. Other members of the family, Larry, Judy, Donna, and David, not only endured inconveniences imposed on them but served as copyists so that the work on extended trips could be accomplished in the limited time available. Larry spent much of three summers and Judy parts of two at the typewriter in this service. The author alone is responsible for the conception of the work and the flaws which may be found in it.

Chapter I
THE DEVELOPMENT AND MANAGEMENT
OF THE RELIGIOUS NEWSPAPER

The area known as the Old Northwest passed from a wilderness territory to an economically and politically decisive region from 1800 to 1860. New states entered the Union in steady progression from the original territory: Ohio in 1803, Indiana in 1816, Illinois in 1818, Michigan in 1837, and Wisconsin in 1848. By 1850 its population included the varied elements from other regions of the United States and from abroad. Population density, including several thriving urban communities, rivaled that of the Northeast and exceeded that of the South. The Northwest held a political balance which first threatened and then helped forcibly to preserve the Union. Its farmers produced more wheat, corn, beef, and pork than farmers of all other sections combined. The Northwest was vitally related to the industrial growth of the young nation as a producer of goods and a source of raw materials and markets fully integrated with the Northeast by the transportation revolution.

Proponents of all of America's religions sought confidently to capture this dynamic region and to shape from it a future for the United States as a fully Christianized nation prepared to teach the entire world the will of God and the ways of political democracy. The religious newspaper seemed to the representatives of the churches to be one of the most promising instruments of conquest available to them. Americans generally were already enthusiastically devoted to the rapidly developing technology of the printed word, especially as it related to weekly and daily newspapers.[1] Some of the clergy were ecstatic. "A well conducted religious periodical is like a thousand preachers, flying in almost as many directions, by means of horses, mailstages, steam boats, rail road cars, ships, etc., etc., offering life and salvation to the sons of men in

1

almost every clime."[2] For scores of ministers with this vision the press, not the pulpit, was to be the "widest channel through which thoughts would be communicated to the millions."[3]

The uniqueness of the *antebellum* religious newspaper was in its blend of secular and religious purposes. For most churchmen, the object involved far more than the proportion of religious material or the mere grafting onto the secular content of newspapers "religious principles and aims."[4] The religious newspaper was an organ which gave not "merely religious intelligence, but a *news* paper, complete in every department of general news, yet upon a religious, instead of a political or literary basis."[5] It was to be an agent in the sanctification of the whole vastness and variety of American life, especially the western part of it, as God's domain. "Let theology, law, medicine, politics, literature, art, science, commerce, trade, architecture, agriculture—in fine, all questions which concern and secure the welfare of a people—be freely discussed and treated, and this, too, for God, for Jesus Christ, and the advancement of the Redeemer's kingdom among men."[6] The religious newspaper "surveys the world not with the eye of the politician, or the merchant, but condenses, arranges, and reports the events of the day, as connected with the religion of Jesus Christ."[7] The news itself had its moral and its gospel, the news sheet being nothing less than "the horologue of Providence."[8]

This grandness of design did not interfere with more mundane expectations. In fact, the first newspaper published under religious sponsorship, the Catholic *Michigan Essay* (1809) in Detroit offered itself in its one issue simply to communicate "whatever may be deemed worthy of information."[9] The first newspaper of primarily religious content in the Northwest was published by the Presbyterian, John Andrews, in Chillicothe, Ohio. He felt that his *Weekly Recorder* (1814-1821) was needed to perform very ordinary secular functions while compensating for the shortage of religious personnel in reaching a scattered population in support of Christian orthodoxy in belief and practice.[10]

The *Essay* and the *Recorder* are representative of several primitive ventures in religious journalism before 1830. Issues were very small, appeared irregularly, and were editorially and mechanically imperfect. Equipment was crude, with skills and labor coming from the editor-proprietor and members of his family, all of whom were inexperienced and already absorbed in the demanding tasks of the frontier. Materials were expensive and uncertain of both quality and delivery.[11] Ministers of the Presbyterian, Baptist, Quaker, Methodist, and United Brethren churches fostered these early papers, but denominational interests were muted. The *Delaware Gazette and Religious Informer* (1818-1819) was, reportedly, the result of the combined efforts of a Presbyterian and a Baptist in that Ohio community.[12] Ecumenicity was normal in the West at this early date, with its application to journalism being due in part to the editor's awareness that his own members were too few and too scattered for his paper to survive on a partisan basis, and to his conscious effort to provide the services of a community newspaper.

After its tentative first steps, the institution of religious journalism began to achieve permanence as the Northwest approached the extraordinary growth of the 1830's. Cincinnati had become a center for the distribution of presses and printing supplies so that larger and better papers rolled quickly from the new cylinder machines.[13] The population of Ohio was nearing its first million and Cincinnati was thriving with a citizenry of 25,000. The Western Reserve was filling rapidly even on the eve of the acceleration provided by the completion of the Ohio Canal in 1832. Illinois, especially opposite St. Louis, was another center of substantial growth at this time.[14] The denominations and their agencies were more than keeping pace with these trends. The decade was hardly under way before several thousand copies of religious newspapers published in these population centers were being distributed to the homes of the Northwest while other papers followed immigrants from the East and South.[15]

Not only was religious journalism launched full force in this decade but it also reached its maturity, assuming no significantly new form or purpose after 1840. The issuance of 40,000 weekly and biweekly circulation by that date provided more than enough experience to achieve that result. The typical religious newspaper was now a weekly folio as large as the proprietor could afford or find a press to print, size itself being one of the criteria of success. A few prominent papers such as the *Catholic Telegraph,* the *Oberlin Evangelist,* and later the *Israelite* did, however, retain the quarto form. The mature paper was quite rigidly departmentalized. The front page was devoted to the weightier matters of theology, morality, science, history, and literature. The second page contained the editorial section, correspondence, and news relating to local congregations and denominational agencies. This section was usually further divided under such headings as revivals, missions, and Sunday Schools. The third page was generally secular in content. If the paper printed advertisements, they were placed on the third and fourth pages, since religious newspapers never carried them on the first page as secular papers usually did.[16]

Editors usually classified the columns on page three as to foreign and domestic news with papers in urban areas carrying a column of city items as well. The state and national legislatures were covered under appropriate headings when they were in session. Either page two or page three contained news of religious activity outside the denomination. Market reports, bank note tables, and death and marriage notices rounded out the contents of this page. The fourth page included the poetry corner and some or all of the departments headed parents, family, youth, children, ladies, agriculture, and miscellany. This latter was exactly that. Oddities of no particular significance including tall tales or frontier superstitions found their way into this column. The farm column was used for items relating to household management and food processing, rarely offering much of detailed scientific, mechanical, or economic value. Often special columns appearing anywhere from pages one through four bore headings naming temperance, slavery, or other reform interests. The eight- or sixteen-page papers positioned their material in about the same order. These papers would normally have three columns to the page with quite large type. The folio papers would have as many as eight very closely printed columns to a page, the aim being to get in as much material of the highest quality as possible. The desire for quality was often frustrated but, contrary to the judgment of some, the religious newspapers were usually superior in quality of paper, printing, editing, style, and form to neighboring secular papers, at least until mid-century.[17]

After maturing in form, quality, and mission, religious journalism expanded rapidly in the 1840's in terms of both new issues and circulation. Religious papers achieved a circulation increase of 35%, distributing about 115,000 copies by 1850. Total circulation had increased to well over 200,000 by 1860, with most denominations having at least one more or less stable journal by that date.[18] Only one group, the Jews, came as newcomers into this field after 1850.

The peculiarities of denominational development, organization, and philosophy were essential features of the business arrangements for the religious newspaper, especially after 1830. Some of the characteristics of the institution can best be seen from this perspective. The Plan of Union (1801), the co-operative home missions agency of the Presbyterian and Congregational Churches, had resulted in the founding of more than one hundred churches and two colleges in the Northwest by 1830.[19] Newspapers, as with other Plan of Union endeavors, were preponderantly Presbyterian in the final analysis. Division into Old and New Schools after 1839 and the existence of the smaller Free and Associate Presbyterians dissipated the concentrated strength of the Presbyterians themselves. Their first and strongest papers emerged in the Western Reserve and in Cincinnati. The *Ohio Observer* (1827-1855) changed locations on the Reserve, experiencing fifteen changes of management during its twenty-nine years. Though an important paper, it never issued more than 2,000 weekly, a circulation it attained in 1833.[20] *The Cincinnati Journal* (1828-1839) and its successor, the *Watchman of the Valley* (1840-1869), as New School organs were relatively more successful, although these papers went through sixteen changes of ownership in one twenty-year period. The former reached 3,600 in 1833 and the latter 4,000 by 1860.[21] The Old School maintained the *Presbyterian of the West* (1841-1869) which had a circulation of 2,800 by 1860.[22] The relative strength of these papers follows closely the distribution of the membership of the contending factions in the Northwest.

The variety and instability of business arrangements reflect the financial burdens which fell on those individuals who conducted this enterprise. Solicitations among the lay and clerical brethren and frequent changes of ownership were ways of distributing initial costs and subsequent losses in those fellowships, such as the Presbyterian and Baptist, which did not have centralized control and financing. Heavy personal losses were very common among proprietors in all denominations in keeping this vital service alive. One of the early proprietor-editors of the *Watchman of the Valley,* not untypically, lost up to $4,000, his entire accumulation of property, during his brief tenure.[23] Those with republican or congregational polity often used the joint stock arrangement to distribute the financial burden. Although both clergy and laymen were sometimes involved, most of the burden fell on the clergy in spite of the fact that they were rarely affluent. Many of the ministers who pledged themselves to buy shares in a company or to pay a portion of a continuing subsidy, under the impact of a sense of duty to the enterprise, overextended themselves and later proved unable or unwilling to keep the commitment. In such cases, the person or persons with the most direct responsibility for the operation had to make up the difference if the paper were to continue.

In view of these difficulties, the Presbyterians at times considered the possibility of consolidating their newspapers or centralizing their control in order to avoid the internal competition which threatened even their strongest weeklies. They emphatically rejected this suggestion, however, in favor of privately or synodically sponsored papers with even the latter the responsibility of a few ministers. Western editors were particularly jealous to safeguard provincial interests but their very resistance to centralization helped to promote it. When the editor announced the sale of the *Ohio Observer* to the *New York Evangelist* he lamented: "It yields to the current, and goes to swell the tide of centralization, of metropolitanism.... Local papers which nourish independence are put by."[24] The New York paper had already fallen heir to the *Christian Journal* in 1839 and the *Chicago Evangelist* (1853-1855) in 1855. Though proliferation of their newspapers was deplored by every Presbyterian editor and the consolidation of western papers was often recommended, it never materialized and, as a result, this family of churches did not have one self-sustaining paper in the Northwest before 1860.

The failure of the Plan of Union produced the *Congregational Herald* (1853-1861) as it had the *Chicago Evangelist*. A group of Chicago pastors founded and

7

managed the *Herald* for 2,500 subscribers in Illinois, Indiana, Wisconsin, and Michigan.[25] Also in the Congregational tradition, the staff of Oberlin College published the biweekly *Oberlin Evangelist* (1838-1852). The *Evangelist* carried less secular material than most such papers, perhaps because its circulation pattern was unique. A large number of its 5,000 subscribers in 1839 were in 1,492 communities in New England, New York, and Pennsylvania.[26]

The Universalists appeared with their first and only prolonged success, the *Star of the West* (1827-1880) in Cincinnati. Universalists had something of a monopoly of ideology among dissenting Protestants in the West, somewhat as the Unitarians in the East. They had sixteen churches in Ohio by 1830 with their most fruitful years in growth and publishing activities in the 1840's when there was a total of 163 organized congregations in Ohio alone.[27] Universalists published many other small papers also under individual auspices, but nearly all of them were eventually bought by the proprietors of the *Star*. The *Star* had 7,000 subscribers by 1852, many of them outside the denomination.[28]

John Mason Peck, minister, farmer, gazetteer, educator, and editor established the first Baptist paper in the Northwest with the financial help of some eastern friends. His *Pioneer of the Valley of the Mississippi* (1829-1838) at Rock Springs, Illinois, had fewer than 1,000 paying subscribers when he sold it to the *Baptist Banner* in Louisville.[29] Baptist journalism had about the same range of types of ownership as the Presbyterian with a corresponding turnover in personnel. These circumstances prompted a frustrated Baptist to inquire, "Which policy in this thing is the wisest and which the best, the Baptist or the Methodist?"[30] This question had followed a comparison of the number and strength of the Methodist and Baptist newspapers in the Northwest. The only official Methodist newspapers in English circulated a total of about 40,000 copies weekly at the time, while five struggling Baptist papers ranged from fewer than 1,000 to 6,000 subscribers with a combined total of no more than 16,000. Baptist papers had a slightly higher ratio of circulation to membership, about one in six to the Methodist one in eight, but they were so dispersed that each paper was financially weak. The *Christian Times,* whose editor made this observation, was, in fact, the only Baptist paper in the region which was approaching both solvency and permanence by 1860.

A committee of the Ohio State Convention presided only briefly over the *Journal and Messenger* (1831-1920), with its final home in Cincinnati. It characteristically absorbed many weaker papers and changed hands often. In spite of being the oldest and most important continuing paper for Baptists, it was circulating only 2,000 in 1836 and 3,000 in 1850.[31] The *Michigan Christian Herald* (1842-1867), also briefly a state convention property represented in the management by a publishing committee, was a relatively successful and well-edited paper which circulated 3,000 copies among 13,000 members in 1858.[32]

The procedures of the Methodist Episcopal Church could rarely be copied, in spite of the envy of other proprietors, because they were directly related to polity. The General Conference decided when a paper was both necessary and practical, selected the most promising location, and then placed the concentrated resources of the denomination behind it. The Methodist Church presented not only much the largest constituency of any group but had an army of itinerant ministers instructed specifically to act as agents in selling and collecting for subscriptions. The ministers were to receive their own papers at reduced rates plus a commission of 40c on a $2.00 subscription, later reduced to 25c on $1.50. The minister's retirement fund was also to receive the profits from the papers, so that the incentives were substantial.[33]

The results were two highly successful official papers,

the *Western Christian Advocate* (1834-1939) in Cincinnati and the *Northwestern Christian Advocate* (1853-1939) in Chicago. Within seventeen months of its founding, the *Western Advocate* had 5,500 patrons, was out of debt, had cash in hand, and physical assets worth $1,000. By 1840, 14,000 took the paper, which gave it the largest circulation of any paper of any type in the region and several times its nearest religious competitor. It had more than doubled this figure by 1860.[34] The Chicago paper was hardly less successful, though it was delayed beyond the normal discretion of the General Conference by a recession and the expensive financial settlement with the Methodist Episcopal Church, South. This delay had led to the founding of unauthorized private ventures in Illinois and Michigan.

The Methodist Protestant press operated, at first, on the basis of individual ownership in keeping with that group's break with traditional Methodist polity. The *Methodist Correspondent* (1830-1836) struggled for a few years before being replaced by the *Western Recorder* (1839-1939) of Zanesville, Ohio. The General Conference later purchased the paper and published it as the *Western Methodist Protestant,* which had 2,930 subscribers among a limited constituency by 1856.[35]

The only denominations to parallel the polity and business arrangement of the Methodist Episcopal Church were the Evangelical Association and the United Brethren Church. The *Religious Telescope* (1835-1946) and the *Deutsche Telescope* (1846-1946) of Circleville, Ohio, were published by order of the General Conference of the United Brethren and placed under the supervision of elected trustees. The English paper had 11,443 patrons and the German paper 1,838 in 1857.[36] Those in the Evangelical Association who were in charge of the *Christliche Botschafter* [*Christian Messenger*] (1836-1946) and the *Evangelical Messenger* (1848-1946), brought to Cleveland from New Berlin, Pennsylvania, in 1854, were directly amenable to the General Conference until 1859. The *Botschafter* reached 5,500 in 1854 while the *Messenger* was still circulating only 4,200 in 1860.[37] These were the only newspapers published by the two groups and they saturated their largely northern constituencies to the extent that about one member in five, or nearly every family, received at least one of the papers. While securely established, the publishing enterprise in these churches did experience financial strain, and it is inconceivable that any papers could have been provided except through this concentration of resources.

The Catholics began publishing the *Telegraph* (1831-   ) in Cincinnati as a diocesan organ closely supervised by the hierarchy. The *Telegraph* was the only permanent, English weekly for Catholics in the antebellum Northwest and the earliest continuing Catholic paper in the United States.[38] Its circulation was only 850 in 1837, but by 1850, enjoying the fruits of immigration, it had expanded to 8,000.[39] At times, the Catholics used the association plan to subsidize their newspapers, but a succession of individual proprietors suggests the same difficulties that other churches had. The sources of the necessary subsidies are obscure. Revealing the financial strain normal to this enterprise, the publisher threatened in 1852 that if he had to borrow any more money he would suspend the *Telegraph,* "to the great joy of our opponents, red-Republicans, Methodists and all that sort of people."[40]

The newspaper enterprise of the Protestant Episcopal Church in the Northwest centered around Kenyon College in Gambier, Ohio. The *Gambier Observer* (1830-1868) was frequently suspended and always in financial difficulty while a series of proprietors lost much personal property in its management. The largest circulation of the *Observer* was 1,200 in 1841. As late as 1855 it had as few as 960 subscribers, with 664 of those among 5,000 communicants in Ohio.[41]

The association of the *Gambier Observer* with a denominational school is typical of a large class of religious newspapers. Several factors encouraged this arrangement. In no case were proprietors or editors trained for or experienced in journalism, and school personnel were better qualified generally for the conduct of a paper than was the average minister. Labor could also be conveniently shared by persons concentrated in one location. Student labor was a consciously sought advantage, for it lifted the load of routine work from those who already had heavy demands on their time and it afforded a means of self-help for college students. Colleges and seminaries often had space and sometimes even publishing facilities of their own or found it convenient to acquire them. Schools also attracted denominational leaders and were otherwise strategic centers of denominational interests. Even though this arrangement rarely improved the financial base, it did provide more stability in staff arrangements. In 1858, after twenty years of publication, the *Oberlin Evangelist* still had all of the original founders on its staff.[42]

Several Lutheran papers were associated with schools in the West, including the most prominent of them, the *Lutheran Standard* (1842-   ), often staffed by college and seminary personnel from Capital University in Columbus, Ohio. The paper relied on a variety of sources of money to make it available to its 1,400 patrons in 1856. The German Reformed *Western Missionary* (1848-1867), with its circulation of 2,200 in 1857, had only a brief association with Heidelberg College in Tiffin, Ohio, but a German paper, the *Evangelist* (1857-1864) was published by a professor there.[43]

Most periodicals among the Disciples and related groups were monthly issues. Their first newspaper, the *Gospel Herald* (1843-1868), which moved about in Ohio, was published under the auspices of a convention of the Christian denomination in behalf of groups in Ohio and

Indiana. The *Christian Age* (1845-1858), after many changes of ownership, was absorbed into the *American Christian Review* (1856-1883) in Cincinnati. The *Review* was uniquely successful for its proprietor and editor, Benjamin Franklin, not simply because of his subscription list of 6,000 but because he was very firm in dropping nonpaying subscribers.[44]

The only Jewish newspapers appeared in Cincinnati under the personal management of the Reformed leader, Isaac Mayer Wise. The English paper was the *Israelite* (1854-   ) and the German paper was known as *Die Deborah* (1855-1899) and was addressed to "the daughters of Israel" who presumably did not have occasion to learn English as soon as their husbands. The former reached a printing of 2,000 by 1855 and the latter 1,800 by 1860. The Jewish constituency in the area was very small, there being no more than eight congregations in Ohio by 1860. Wise received numerous "very glowing promises, which, however, were never kept" in behalf of his enterprise that apparently received its subsidy from a publishing business which his brother-in-law, Edward Bloch, conducted in partnership with Wise.[45]

Foreign language papers, largely German and Scandinavian, formed a very significant portion of the denominational press in this region. Two distinct groups of such papers developed. The first and largest consisted of papers designed for that part of church membership not yet having made the transition to the English language. Although these papers were not useful in helping individuals learn the language, editors did otherwise seek to help the immigrant adjust to his new surroundings as well as to guide him through the perils to his original faith in America's competitive religious environment. To these ends, they emphasized news from the old country for its emotional value and domestic items which would familiarize the reader with politics and education, along with economic opportunities and risks in the new country.[46] They were even inclined toward explicit advice as to election alternatives.

These features were especially true of the Norwegians and Swedes who made almost no distinction between secular and religious items when their newspapers first appeared in the 1850's in northern Illinois and Wisconsin. This condition grew out of the fact that religious considerations figured in the migration and the fact that pastors exercised leadership in all aspects of public life.[47] One early Norwegian paper, the *Emigraten,* was referred to as "the clergymen's paper," for, although entirely political, the association which published it consisted exclusively of pastors.[48] The *Kirke Tidende* ... [*Church Journal*] (1851-1854) and the *Norsk Lutherske Tidende* ... [*Norwegian Lutheran Church Journal*] (1857-1860) emerged as the major religious papers of the Norwegians. After a period of evolution toward a separate religious paper, *Det Ratta Hemlandet* [*The True Homeland*] (1855-1869) became the principal organ of the Swedish Lutherans. *Hemlandet* had about 800 subscribers in the late 1850's.[49]

The Catholics established their first German weekly in the United States, *Der Wahrheitsfreund* [*Friend of Truth*] (1837-1907), in Cincinnati under the same auspices as the *Telegraph.* This paper also became the first Catholic daily in the country when it went to that frequency from 1846-1850.[50] The German Catholic press followed the heavy German migration to Chicago and Milwaukee with several durable papers both religious and secular.[51] The Catholics pioneered less successfully in journalism for French Canadians along the Great Lakes and the rivers of Illinois with the *Citoyen* (1850-1851) in Detroit and *Le Journal de L'Illinois* (1857-1863).[52]

The Evangelical Association, of German origin, was slow in making the transition to English. Their original paper, the *Botschafter,* was published twelve years before their English paper. In contrast, the United Brethren anglicized quickly and published the weak *Deutsche*

Telescope as a concession to a minority.[53] The German papers of the Lutherans, Reformed, and the Jews also fit this category.

The second distinctive group of foreign language papers was designed for proselytizing among German and Scandinavian minorities. Those who published papers in the native tongue in order to protect a national faith often put their readers on guard against predators. The founding of several subsidized foreign language papers supported the wisdom of that warning. The Methodists raised $2,400 in a special campaign to issue *Der Christliche Apologete* [*Christian Advocate*] (1839-1941) in Cincinnati when only 100 charter subscribers were available. The dynamic and talented German immigrant, editor William Nast, pursued German rationalists and German Catholics with equal zeal in order to create a German constituency for Methodism. By 1855 he had a circulation of 6,175.[54]

The Methodists approached the Swedes through a mixed-purpose paper, which continued into the twentieth century, called *Sändebudet* [*Messenger*] beginning in 1862 in Rockford.[55] Baptists briefly sought after the Swedes through the *Friheitsvännen* [*Friend of Liberty*] (1859-1861) from Galesburg[56] and the Universalists even more briefly published an overture to the Germans, the *Lichtfreund* [*Friend of Light*] in 1840 in Cincinnati.[57] In a business characterized by insolvency, these ventures were especially precarious.

Whatever the purposes of a paper and under whatever business arrangements, the denominational newspaper was rarely a financial success. The most important source of a paper's income, at least after cash donations and other subsidies, was paid subscriptions. Proprietors employed various devices to enlist paying readers, the most common being simply to try to instill the same zeal for the religious newspaper in their readers as the proprietors and editors themselves had. Each reader, and especially the clerical reader, was assumed to be a missionary for the paper. The few more affluent and highly organized projects might have the services of a full-time traveling agent whose task was to visit conventions and churches throughout the denomination in behalf of subscriptions. Bonuses, usually in the form of books, might be offered to anyone who solicited a given number of readers, or they might be offered as an inducement to pay large accounts. Proprietors kept their readers informed constantly of the advantages of paying the cash price in advance.

To insure the largest possible number of readers, proprietors deliberately kept rates low. They were normally $1.00 and occasionally $1.50 in advance for a semimonthly paper and $2.00 to $2.50 for weeklies. Credit generally increased the costs by $1.00 or more a year. Higher rates were exceptional and usually involved papers published early in the century when expenses were very high, although there were a few other exceptions such as the *Israelite,* always $3.00 in advance. The Methodist *Christian Advocates* were reduced, on the other hand, to $1.50. This price expanded the circulation, but it reduced the profits which were to go into the ministerial retirement fund.

At all times within the period before the Civil War, some proprietors advertised that they would accept commodities at market value in lieu of cash. The proprietor of the *Weekly Recorder* announced that he would receive "fire wood, beef, pork, corn, vegetables, etc." or "Clean Linen and Cotton Rags, at three cents a pound." Subscribers to the *Western Intelligencer* received an extension beyond seed time when it would become more convenient to get their grain to the agents. The Quaker *Philanthropist* named the mills in the area at which wheat could be applied to the indebtedness of subscribers.[58]

As late as 1846, the editor of the *Religious Telescope* reminded his rural readers that winter was due and firewood was needed in the office. "We want none but such as can be made suitable for stoves." A Baptist proprietor in Chicago asked that those subscribers who had requested the privilege of paying in wood "bring us some immediately." In the rural context of Norwegian settlement it was natural for the proprietor of *Kirke Tidende* to "accept flour, potatoes, butter, meat, etc.... at top market prices." Again the stipulation was "just send it to us immediately."[59]

This sense of immediacy was not limited to these pleas for commodities. Many readers simply did not pay for their papers, and churchmen universally recognized the credit system as the blight of religious newspaper publishing. The normally severe financial straits of the papers made payments of subscriptions always an urgent matter. The admirable devotion and sacrifice of proprietors and editors was, in consequence, often diluted by symptoms of self-righteousness and self-pity and by bitterness and recriminations. They dunned incessantly through the editorial columns and sometimes these duns were accompanied by threats, unfavorable comments on the integrity of readers, and by lectures on morality.[60] These men were, of course, not only dependent on payment of subscriptions for a living, but many had risked personal funds from other sources which were threatened if the enterprise failed. Having sacrificed so extensively themselves, it was a special problem to understand a reader who could not or would not pay $1.00 or $2.00 for the good of the cause, whether he liked the paper or not.

The simple expedient of dropping a subscriber who had not paid was rarely used. The result was the accumulation of enormous arrearages along with a festering relationship with the public. The *Ohio Observer* showed arrearages of $3,000 at the end of its third year from a list of 2,000. Some owed as much as $12 each. Within another decade the total arrearages had grown to $7,000. The *Christian Times,* reflecting in part the panic of 1857, gave as its accumulated arrearages nearly $12,000, among a circulation of 6,000. The *Religious Telescope,* presumably on the cash system in 1858, reported delinquent subscriptions totaling $19,167 over a period of twenty years.[61] Far more serious was the delinquency for one small paper of one half of a list of 620 in one year.[62] The *Catholic Telegraph* reported 841 delinquent among 1,200 subscribers for one volume.[63] As amazing as these arrearages were, they existed among those papers sufficiently healthy to survive long enough to leave a record behind them.

Rather than impugn readers' motives or to imply the threat of legal action, many editors published a "black list" of those who were in arrears. This might be done for the benefit of agents, as a form of punishment, or as a warning to other publishers.[64] Proprietors occasionally tried to cope with delinquent accounts by using agents or a professional agency service. This method was never successful. One owner sent out an agent with accounts of several hundred dollars and he returned with $14.[65] Professional collectors received from 75c to $1.00 per subscription, leaving considerably less than a profit for the owner.[66] The only useful agency system was that based on the voluntary services of the pastors in the field and, except where this was regularized and accompanied by substantial incentives as in the Methodist Church, it was uncertain in results.

The failure of threats and professional attention left only the unwelcome alternative of going to a strictly cash system. Benjamin Franklin of the *American Christian Review* was among the more businesslike. "Our terms of subscription," he wrote, "are not only *professedly,* but *actually, cash in advance.*" A red mark on a paper indicated an expiration date two or three weeks hence. "If the time expires and the money does not come we take it *as a modest hint that the paper is not wanted.*"[67] Even the Methodist Church did not fully apply the cash system until the 1840's, relying on the efficiency of its itinerant system years before the cash system was actually enforced. For the United Brethren it was established by the General Conference at the request of the staff of the *Religious Telescope* in 1845 and duly announced. It was not applied uniformly until 1857 when the editor admitted that the paper had not operated fully within the directive although 2,000 accounts had been erased for delinquency. When the synods in charge of the *Central Christian Herald* acted to put the paper on a cash basis its staff likewise did not firmly apply the rule.[68] Editors and proprietors simply would not dilute their religious mission by giving up subscribers in order to relieve financial strain.

Most religious newspapers attempted to gain financial strength by carrying paid advertisements. It is not possible to determine the revenue derived from them. Rates were the same as for secular weeklies, which varied considerably.[69] Common rates were 50c to 75c a square or $1.00 for three insertions with rapidly diminishing rates for continued printing. These rates could have substantially added to the income of a paper with several twenty-inch columns filled weekly. Most advertisements, however, were either carried at the lowest advertised rates or at much lower contract rates. It is also probable that bills for advertising were not automatically collectible. There is no indication that advertising revenue materially changed the position of these newspapers and where revenues were reported from this source they were negligible. The *Michigan Christian Herald* identified only $40 as advertising revenue from an average of one or two columns in 1843; the *Gambier Observer* $40 in four years; and the *Religious Telescope* $102 in 1847 which included some income from job printing as well.[70]

Noteworthy papers which never did carry advertising were the *Oberlin Evangelist* and the two papers of the Evangelical Association. Official Methodist papers in the West did not carry advertisements until authorized to do so in 1860. The *Religious Telescope* of the United Brethren carried them intermittently. Many proprietors who did carry them injected an arbitrary limit to the space allocated to them, jealously conserving their columns for the less crass content of denominational newspapers. Since advertisements were, for the most part, considered a necessary evil, no more than six or seven columns of a large folio would be allowed and these were always in the rear section.[71]

Some did justify the inclusion of advertisements on grounds other than those of financial necessity. At least nine out of ten of the publishers of religious newspapers thought that their service to the public should be equivalent to all the services of conventional newspapers. Many proprietors considered advertising an essential service, especially early in the history of the enterprise, and were restrained only by the advertising which was available.[72] Many religious papers, 1814-1840, were the only advertising media for the people of a community and this was also true of the foreign language papers at a much later date. William Nast of the *Christliche Apologete* was very proud of the potential of his paper as "the best advertising medium" available to Germans in the West.[73]

The staff of the *Religious Telescope* campaigned in their denomination to get the General Conference to remove restrictions on advertising on the grounds that it would allow the paper to be much larger. The trustees did act to enlarge the paper on the condition that 1,000 new subscribers be enrolled. When that number was reached the *Telescope* appeared proudly in enlarged form with two or three columns of advertising in each issue. The editor pointed out to merchants that the *Telescope* had the largest circulation in Ohio except for a few papers in Cincinnati. With the expenses of the enlargement paid, however, the advertisements were once more dropped as existing contracts expired.[74]

The editors of the Methodist *Christian Advocates* in the West began to argue for advertisements well in advance of receiving permission to carry them. James V. Watson of the *Northwestern Advocate* believed that the appeal of the paper outside the denomination could be considerably enhanced by including them. They could be truthful, he said, and any notion to the contrary was "fanatical and old fogy." Not to advertise was also to cut the paper off from men of commerce. Watson's successor argued that the paper would be more useful to its patrons if he could carry advertising, especially from major cities in the region.[75] Once authorities agreed, the *Northwestern Advocate* devoted one and one half pages to advertisements in its new eight-page edition in 1861.

An even more complicated question followed the decision to carry advertisements, for advertising had to be made to "comport" with religion. To almost all Protestant editors in this epoch, liquor and tobacco were taboo along with theatrical performances and horse races. Only very occasionally did tobacco or some form of liquor for medicinal uses gain a place in the advertisements. On the other hand, public facilities in which liquor was not sold and which remained closed on Sunday, were even singled out editorially. Catholic and Jewish publications did not generally follow these taboos and sometimes even ridiculed some of them.

The major test of moral values came with regard to the quack medicines so abundant at the time. While some papers sold space to the purveyors of these cure-alls without reservation, many refused to do so. The editor of the *Michigan Christian Herald* rather frankly set forth the dilemma for his profession when advertisements of patent medicines were offered. "A few of these have hitherto found a place in the *Herald,* and it is perhaps proper to state, that, as mere business transactions, none are more promptly or liberally paid for. But that is not the only, or the chief consideration of a religious body."[76]

The editor of the *Western Christian Advocate* found

that patent medicine did not have the "intrinsic worth" necessary to qualify as proper advertising for a religious paper any more than did hair dye. The influence of the *Advocate* would never be lent to these "shocking" impositions on the public. The editor of the *Watchman of the Valley* also had reservations. Some patent medicines might be useful, but after much thought he had reached the "conclusion that the system . . . is an alarming and growing evil, a system of imposture and quackery." Inflating his heroism, he wrote that at the risk of the "loss of several hundred dollars" he had decided to drop the advertising of these potions as soon as the contracts expired. The editor of the *Religious Telescope* gave up one advertisement for a "fits" remedy simply because "we think our readers generally have become tired of seeing the same thing in the paper so long."[77]

Two editors exposed the trickery of one clever advertising man who wrote letters describing visits to prominent churches in the East whose pastors showed symptoms of "prospective consumption" while delivering the sermon. The writer was reminded of a new medicine "working wonders in curing consumption, and he took great pleasure in sending the news to the West." The maneuver seduced the editor of the *Christian Age and Sower* who published just such a letter describing a visit to Henry Ward Beecher's church.[78] One of those who exposed this fraud was the editor of the *Presbyterian of the West*. In spite of such a keen sense of rectitude regarding the error of the *Christian Age,* he refused to accept the word of a reader that one of the medicines which he advertised in his own columns was worthless after the reader showed substantial and detailed proof that it was. Out of "fairness" the editor printed the letter of protest but turned down the reader's request to drop the advertisement on the grounds that "the remedy spoken of may nevertheless be as efficient as it professes to be."[79]

The Baptist *Christian Register* gave the strongest criticism of patent medicine advertising and selling. "The Pulpit and the Press are the instructors of the people, and hence are solicited to trump to the public ear the most glaring deceptions—to gratify the money-grasping spirit of the age." He sympathized with those whose money was earned by hard work "while the empiric may take the names of the dead to recommend his nostrums, and by the aid of the religious press, and its hired encomiums, deceives society, ruins health, and accumulates a fortune."[80]

Most editors did not want their readers to consider that carrying an advertisement, whatever the product, implied an endorsement. The proprietor of the German Reformed *Missionary* did, however, bravely announce that readers could assume the truth of any claims made anywhere in his columns. More normal was the Presbyterian's statement to the effect that the advertising department was one that could not be made religious. The readers must determine for themselves by trial and error the veracity of the claims.[81] Another editor indicated that freedom of discussion and opinion applied to advertising so he would not accept responsibility for the truth of anything above someone else's signature.[82]

Occasionally editors endorsed personally some of the products they advertised. This included glowing praise for railroads, especially those which invited ministers on free excursions. These endorsements also included insurance, medical or surgical skills observed by the editor, dental service, stoves, and sewing machines. For some reason, even many who did not otherwise advertise patent medicines not only advertised "Ayer's Cherry Pectoral" but endorsed it editorially. The same extravagant claims, though not quite so universal as to its curative powers, were made for this concoction as for any other patent medicine. Perhaps editors were impressed by the testimonials of well-known doctors, college presidents, college professors, statesmen, and clergymen. This figured at least in the explanations given by editors of the *Prairie Herald, Religious Telescope,* and *Ohio Observer* for their personal endorsement. The close coincidence of dates and very similar endorsements in these papers suggest the possibility of another very clever and concerted advertising campaign,[83] especially since the *Herald* and the *Observer* did not usually publish advertisements of this type.

Almost all of those who supported the religious newspapers financially had done so at a personal loss whatever the original motivation and expectations. This sacrifice is one of the most significant measures of the belief of its promoters in the value of their enterprise. Especially noteworthy are those numerous instances in which one man or a group of men kept on year after year until their personal funds were exhausted and they had borrowed all they could. As important as it was, financial loss was not the only form of sacrifice which made the religious newspaper a reality in the Northwest in this epic period. Editors, who were often proprietors as well, took up a task which was, for the vast majority, a distasteful one and one for which they were ill prepared intellectually, temperamentally, or by experience.

Chapter II
THE EDITORIAL CORPS

The editor was the person most intimately associated with the week-to-week life and unique personality of the religious newspaper. As with all those associated with the enterprise, editors were attracted to it largely by their sense of duty to the gospel and by the vision of an extraordinary extension of their personal influence. Such attractions as the post held were offset, as they quickly discovered, by unending chores and harassments for which they were not prepared. They were also poorly compensated materially for their work, and often not at all. As a result, for a very large number the editorship became an almost intolerable burden, especially in view of their primary commitment to a conventional ministry. In spite of this, the editor invested himself, and often his money, to conduct the enterprise because he thought it was one of the most promising of the age.

The editor came to his post by one of several means. More often than not he was either the sole proprietor or one of several proprietors; hence he combined the burdens of ownership with the burdens of editing. When he was the chief force in organizing a paper, the editor was self-appointed, though probably after much informal urging by his colleagues in the church. In all those instances where denominations controlled the papers at the general level, members of conferences or conventions elected the editors. Otherwise the associations or trustees who supplied the means and who were responsible for the affairs of the paper recruited the editor. The method of selection did not materially affect such denominational relationship as a paper might have. The self-appointed editor was hardly less committed to the goals of his church than the person who owed his tenure to an election in the highest denominational body.

The editorial tenure was not only derived from several

different sources but it varied widely in length. The longest term of service was fifty-four years. This was achieved by William Nast, editor of the Methodist *Christliche Apologete* until his death in 1892; Isaac Wise was nominally if not actively editor of the *Israelite* until his death in 1899; Justin A. Smith was editor of the Baptist *Christian Times* until his death in 1896. Such terms of service were unique. Even Charles Elliott's broken tenure of sixteen years as publisher and editor of the Methodist *Western Advocate* was exceptional. Six to eight years, in fact, was a long term for this position. Editors could seldom afford to offer this service or seldom cared to offer it any longer than that.

Editors of religious newspapers were almost without exception clergymen. There was no alternative in the rules of the Methodist, Evangelical, and United Brethren Churches. College professors often served as editors but they were generally also ordained elders in their churches. George Cole, for several years editor of the Baptist *Cross and Journal,* was an exception to this rule in that as a college professor and businessman he was also an "avowed" layman.[1] Elisha W. Chester was a lawyer before he became editor of the Presbyterian *Cincinnati Journal* and, to recover losses of $7,500, he resumed his practice after he sold the paper.[2] Several Catholic editors were laymen but the editors of the most important Catholic paper, the *Telegraph,* were priests under the direction of their bishop.

The editor was likely to be or to become one of the principals in his denomination. Elliott was the only one of four editors of the *Western Christian Advocate* not to be elected bishop (1834-1860). Even one assistant editor, Leonidas Hamline, moved directly from that post to the bishopric. William W. Orwig was editor at various times of the *Christliche Botschafter* for the Evangelical Association and bishop, 1859-1863. Several editors of the papers of the United Brethren in Christ also became bishops.

Below this level, nearly every editor held one or more other denominational assignments.

The geographical origins of these men were as richly varied as everything else about them. Relatively few were natives of the Northwest and, in fact, many more were born in Europe than in the area itself. In nearly every case the editors of the foreign language papers were foreign-born. A number of the editors of the Evangelical and United Brethren papers, however, were notable exceptions who came usually from Pennsylvania. Several editors of English-language papers came from the British Isles. James V. Watson and Charles Elliott of the two Methodist papers in the West were from England and Ireland respectively. David Edwards of the *Religious Telescope* was from Wales.

Only a few editors came from the southern states, constituting a ratio to the total corps less than the ratio of southerners to the general population. More Presbyterians and Disciples than other groups came from southern states or had at one time lived there. The principal points of origin were New England and New York. Baptists, Universalists, and Congregationalists, consistent with the geographical development of their denominations, appeared in especially large numbers from New England. Methodist editors were the most diverse in origin, Watson and Elliott having come from the British Isles, Nast from Germany, Thomas A. Morris from Virginia, Matthew Simpson and Thomas M. Eddy from Ohio, and Calvin Kingsley from New York.

The level of formal education attained by these editors also varied, although most were educated well above the average level of the population and of their own colleagues. Many, however, served as editors without the benefit of formal education. Isaac Walter of the Christian denomination attended school a total of seventeen months.[3] The Disciples' Benjamin Franklin, in spite of his ancestry, was self-educated and even that process was delayed until he became a minister at the age of twenty-seven.[4] Three of the prominent editors of Methodist Protestant papers had little or no formal education. Asa Shinn was said never to have seen an English grammar prior to becoming a preacher. Ancel Bassett, both editor and historian of his denomination, received what education he had from his mother. Bassett described himself as having received an excellent classical education as a youth by sweeping out a school house. In spite of his lack of formal schooling, Bassett was a student of Greek, an author, and a student of the science of botany.[5]

Many Baptist editors did have college and some even seminary education acquired in the better eastern schools such as Brown and Andover. Although Methodists repudiated seminary training at this time, they exalted college education and most of their editors were college graduates. Kingsley and Simpson had attended Allegheny College; but the best-educated Methodist in the West was William Nast, a German-educated scholar of theology and philosophy and a teacher of languages. Presbyterian editors were more uniformly and better educated than Methodists though many of them, including the leading Old School personality, Nathan Rice, were tutored in theology by older ministers in lieu of institutional training. Some Lutheran editors also received their theological training in America by this arrangement.

There was one aspect of the training of these men which was universal. Neither by education nor experience were they prepared for editing a newspaper. This was also true, of course, for most journalists of the time. In contrast to his secular contemporary, however, the editor of the religious paper did not choose the position for business purposes or because of professional taste. Out of the scores of men who edited religious newspapers in the Northwest only one, Luther Stone of the *Watchman of the Prairies* seems to have come West with such a career specifically in view.

Editorial mobility was a common experience for religious journalists. James B. Walker was associated with the *Ohio Observer* in the Western Reserve, the *Watchman of the Valley* in Cincinnati, and both the *Prairie Herald* and the *Congregational Herald* in Chicago over a period of two decades. Nathan Rice edited at least five papers in different locations: three in or near Cincinnati, one in St. Louis, and one in Chicago. Warren Isham was an editor of the *Ohio Observer*, then the *Michigan Observer*, before he finally became editor of the *Michigan Farmer*. Epaphras Goodman edited the *Cincinnati Journal*, an anti-Catholic paper, and a religious antislavery weekly. The Methodist, Elliot, began his editorial career with the *Pittsburgh Conference Journal* which became the *Pittsburgh Christian Advocate*. He was editor of the *Western Christian Advocate*, 1836-1848, and again, 1852-1856. In the interim he was asked to teach languages at McKendree College and to edit the *Illinois Christian Advocate*. He became editor of the *Central Christian Advocate* in St. Louis in 1860. During most of this time as editor, Elliott complained frequently about the onerous nature of his job. Universalist editors were especially migratory in their habits and, although there was an exceptionally large number of Universalist papers over a period of time, there were relatively few editors.

The editing of a religious newspaper was very demanding of time and energy, especially for men who rarely considered this the work for which they were suited or to which they were originally committed. On some of the more prosperous papers such as those of the Methodist Church, assignments were divided. The denomination even provided an assistant editor for the *Western Christian Advocate* much of the time to do the routine work of getting out an issue. But this was not typical. Most editors complained repeatedly of an excessive work load in relation to the paper itself and to the additional responsibilities they carried as pastors, educators, denominational administrators, and managers of a farm or business. The editor of such an important paper as the New School *Central Christian Herald* reported as late as 1858 that he had been forced by circumstances to assume the financial management of the paper in addition to editorial duties. In connection with the paper's indebtedness and its arrearages, he had sent 200 letters by his own hand within two weeks in addition to all other labor on the weekly.[6] The editor of a small Baptist paper in Illinois had earned his year's compensation of $50 in profits only because he had himself folded, wrapped, and addressed 800-900 copies each two weeks. In addition, he had a particularly time-demanding congregation under his care and he was an active member of the Board of the General Association. His personal life was also burdensome in that his wife had been ill and required his close personal attention.[7] Many of these editors either had congregations under their care or were otherwise preaching regularly.

W. W. Eaton, editor of the *Christian Age* in 1855, claimed that he had "labored more intensely than during any former year" of his life in the past twelve months. He had worked fifteen hours a day for the publication, missionary, and Bible Society interests of the Disciples. With his own hands he had marked books, sold them, and kept accounts for the book store. He had furnished material for three printers, proofread for two of the publications, and supervised every department of the publishing enterprise. He had received and read 2,000-3,000 letters and had written 650. He was publishing and financial agent in charge of issuing new books, contracts, and bookbinding arrangements. He had attended social meetings, board and society meetings, and he had preached nearly every Sunday. Among all these activities he had sandwiched the editorial responsibility for a substantial weekly paper, deferring most editorial writing until after 10:00 at night. He thought that his work load was an adequate apology "for our many blunders and deficiencies."[8]

Much earlier in this epoch John Mason Peck had also issued his paper under the pressure of multiple duties. He was author, manager of varied publishing interests, denominational leader, educator, politician, and owner of a farm from which he probably derived most of his living. He had to suspend temporarily his *Pioneer* in July, 1837, while he spent several days in his harvest. The *Pioneer* was costing twice as much as he was receiving on it; hence he could not afford to hire a harvest hand.[9] Some years later, a Methodist Protestant editor in Ohio had much the same problem. In August of 1843 he was securing his harvest on the farm where his press and office were housed. During the same month he had gone to Pittsburgh for the General Conference, then, in September, to a neighborhood camp meeting and to the Muskingham Annual Conference. In October he had harvested his apple crop from which he sold 140 barrels at a profit of $100. His office was "ankle deep with papers and letters," many dealing with urgent matters. To those who objected to his neglect, he pointed out that the paper depended on his income rather than the reverse; hence $100 from his farm was as vital for his readers as for himself.[10]

In addition to their larger burden of time, there were the countless hazards and petty annoyances of which editors often complained in rather personal terms to their subscribers. Unreliable mail delivery was a frequent complaint, and the post office and sometimes its local personnel would be editorially chastised.[11] Sickness of the editor or members of his family or his staff often delayed publication or resulted in an abbreviated issue. The annual summer epidemics of intestinal disorders in Cincinnati were usually reflected in a diminishing of the editorial service. An aged assistant editor was gored by a bull almost to the point of death and used the occasion after his recovery to describe his injuries in vivid detail and to warn readers "against putting too much confidence in dangerous animals and being off their watch while near them."[12] The printing trade seemed to have had a special attraction for men with a wanderlust and an appetite for liquor, with embarrassing results in terms of meeting publishing deadlines.[13] The uncertain quality of paper and the uncertainty of its arrival were problems. An editor complained of a shortage of presses in Chicago and, not having his own press at the time, he had to wheel the composed paper several blocks.[14] A Norwegian editor had to take his copy twelve miles and, as a result, there was no opportunity at all for proofreading. He acknowledged that this makeshift arrangement left the reader to guess at the content of his paper.[15] One editor experienced a delay when the ceiling fell on his press and type.[16] This mishap could be classed as an act of God but that which befell James Watson's office could not. It was generally assumed that the whiskey sellers of Adrian were responsible for breaking into his office and destroying the account books and the mailing list of the *Michigan Christian Advocate*.[17] Watson was, among other things, an outstanding lecturer and writer on the subject of temperance. He did his editorial and other work for a decade under the handicap of an unusually severe asthmatic condition which rendered him an invalid much of the time. Certainly one of the most unusual complaints came from an editor of the *Central Christian Herald*. He had an especially difficult time with an issue since he could find so little of interest to publish. "There is literally nothing stirring. Business is dull, religion is dead, even politics are creating no excitement, and nothing seems to flourish but wickedness. We hope to see better times."[18]

The editorial responsibility for a large weekly or semimonthly was a demanding task without the major frustration of other duties and petty annoyances. One of the most important chores was, of course, the conduct of the editorial column. Original editorial matter varied according to the editors' personal inclinations and the issues at hand. Their overriding problem was time. "To express our opinion on passing events in such manner as will answer the purposes for which this paper was established requires time," wrote an editor. "Were it not for our labors at the mechanical part of the business we might express our opinions in writing."[19] Even when an editor began to develop a theme in his column, it was likely to be postponed or abandoned because of a traveling assignment or other pressing duties which required him to leave the work with his family or someone else.[20]

James Watson thought that four-fifths of the editor's time should be devoted to preparing for and writing editorials. "The editorial is the brain of a paper.... It is the leaders, energised with living thought, clothed in all the panoply of its powers that constitute the Urim and Thummim character of the high priests of journalism."[21] Elliott, in Cincinnati, bemoaned the fact that routine work took time from the study and the meditation which was the essential preliminary to editorial writing.[22] A Presbyterian editor, in underscoring the importance of the editorial to him, wrote that the loss of his life savings on a religious newspaper was not important to him in view of the fact that the editorial column had given "a feeble man, whose spirit far outstripped his powers,... the opportunity to hurl, at the enemy of all unrighteousness in our land, the shafts of truth, with more effect than from any other position he has ever occupied."[23]

In spite of such interest in the editorial, much of the content of the religious newspaper was not original, but consisted of selections clipped from a variety of periodicals. Secular news was nearly always gathered thus, most of the religious news, and most of the material in the specialized departments ranging in content from theology and science to useless trivia. Thus much of editors' time

33

was devoted to extracting from a vast quantity of printed matter that fraction of material best for inclusion in the editors' papers. One man complained that this involved much reading "for nothing."[24] Some of this material was used as it was and some was altered. Watson estimated that he reworked 100 or more paragraphs of this miscellaneous material taken from fifty papers, edited twenty-five manuscripts, and proofread the sheet at least three times for each weekly issue.[25]

Since so much material came from other journals, the issue of plagiarism arose frequently. Everyone engaged in the same practice and editors even exchanged papers with each other as a mutual favor. Most of the content of the newspapers of the time was considered a part of the public domain. Even so, editors identified the sources of much of the material. In general, plagiarism was not considered unethical, although editors did frequently, but usually gently, chide their fellow editors when they borrowed editorials or other articles without credit. Editors also had to warn contributors who might submit a piece as their own only to have the editor discover later, to his great chagrin, that it was purloined from another paper.[26]

After the selected items, editors filled most of the space with contributed items, though this material was often disappointing in both quantity and quality. Among the reasons offered in favor of regional or local newspapers was that they would encourage the clergy of the area to write, thus developing their intellectual and literary ability. Probably more appealing to them was the argument that the printed word would give influence to their views. In spite of this, it was very common for editors to complain about the lack of suitable manuscripts and to encourage the constituent clergy to help them fill their pages. The clergy of the Evangelical Association, and quite possibly in other cases as well, were reluctant to write for their papers because they did not want to offend their more conservative colleagues nor did they want to appear to be victims of pride for trying to get their names in print.[27] The majority of churchmen were not as reserved as these perfectionist brethren. The readers contributed several categories of material to their editors. Theoretically, nothing of the paper's content was outside this possibility if the writer had any news or was knowledgeable in a particular area. The general articles on the front page might be contributed or selected but preferably the former. Denominational news included local items from pastors of churches and denominational activities reported by leaders of various agencies. Items on temperance, slavery, and other reforms might be contributed. Nearly all of the large papers used regional and even foreign contacts as correspondents who wrote more or less regularly of religious and political activities from their communities. The Methodist *Advocates* especially had a highly developed system of such correspondents, as did some of the more important Presbyterian papers.

Marriage and death notices were also numbered among contributed items. Editors had special problems with death notices, chief among them being their number and length. Editors were too jealous of space for material of general appeal to want to print elaborate eulogies of those who were strangers to most readers. Occasionally, denominational bodies even imposed restrictions on editors concerning the length and content of obituaries. One editor did not feel secure in printing elaborate praises of the deceased since "nothing is more common than fulsome panegyric, or extravagant praise" under those circumstances.[28] Mundane details of a person's life such as his marriage date or his change of residence were not worthy of public notice. "It is the religious experience and the dying exercises that the public look for in all memoirs and obituaries."[29] It was, of course, precisely these matters that required the most space to describe.

Editors published advice freely for their potential contributors. One can construct a composite list inclusive of the variety of advice offered which, had it been followed, would have saved the editor much labor. 1. Be brief and precise since space is at a premium and long articles are not likely to be read anyway. 2. Concentrate on religious news such as accounts of revivals, the activities of churches, and of denominational agencies. 3. Present controversial material, if at all, fairly and courteously, without indulging in personalities or ridicule or abusive language. 4. A contribution must be accompanied by the name of the author though he may request that it not be published. 5. Write grammatically, logically, and with due regard for use of the dictionary, for spelling, and for punctuation. Revise and refine articles before sending them. 6. *"Watch, and fortify yourselves against the temptation of sending any poetry to the editor."*[30]

The latter two especially gave editors many dreary hours. Editing articles submitted by poorly educated first- or second-generation Americans was especially difficult and irritating. The editor of the *Evangelical Messenger* was surprised and disappointed that his contributors were not making more rapid progress in improving their English. "Come, brethren," he exhorted, "this will not do! All the world is now moving at the speed of *steam* and *lightning*, and we dare not stay behind, in regard to knowledge and literature. . . . Hunt up your grammars and dictionaries, your inkstand, pen and paper, and set yourselves to work, in good earnest!"[31] Another editor similarly situated complained because he was criticized, accurately, for grammatical errors in his paper. He claimed that much of the material submitted to him was so badly written that it was almost impossible to correct all the mistakes. However "shockingly ungrammatical" some of the material was when finally printed, he had done as much "as any living editor in correcting manuscript."[32] One editor gave an example of the type of material he received from nearly illiterate and, in this case, irate readers. "Nor I Wont pay out Money for to uphold Such a old Rip as you air it tis not for the good of Peoples Souls you Publish Such papers as you don you old sCamp."[33]

Every editor had a surplus of poetry in his desk. This excess accounts for the admonition by one editor, "Let rhyme writing alone. The market is drugged." He further advised those who could not restrain their impulse to write poems to "creep off softly into the woods and read them to the squirrels and birds. In this way you will have much more of enjoyment than by writing verses and sending them for some poor editor to examine." This same individual estimated that he could not publish more than one in fifty of the contributions.[34] Editors did publish contributed poetry regularly on religious, sentimental, moral, practical, and social themes, depending on the editor's taste or his understanding of the readers' tastes. The sentiment of the poetry had priority over its literary quality. One editor published a poem under this priority but counseled the author to stop wasting his time trying to develop an ability God had not given him.[35]

At least one man did not share the usual impatience with poetry and poets. T. M. Eddy, a Methodist, defended poets from charges of eccentricity and defended poetry as "the highest style of thought. It is philosophy, or history, or sentiment on fire." He used William Cullen Bryant and Henry Wadsworth Longfellow as examples of men who were both poets and men of affairs.[36] Editors frequently published selections from these two as well as from John Greenleaf Whittier, whose themes they often found attractive. All editors could and did use such poems as Bryant's "The Snow Shower," Longfellow's "Woods in Winter," or Whittier's "Life," and some even took delight in Edgar Allen Poe's "The Raven."

The burdensome features of an editor's work might have been ameliorated somewhat if he had received adequate compensation. Instead, the anxiety created by financial problems of his own frequently compounded his woes. Those denominations which published papers under their general supervision paid editors a fixed salary. No specific figures are available for Methodist editors but there is every indication that their salaries were among the highest and entirely adequate. Annual salaries ranged from $150 in the 1830's to $650 in the 1850's. In 1847, the Evangelical Association paid their editor $225 plus $15 for each child in his home under fourteen.[37] United Brethren pastors kept close watch over their editor's salary lest it exceed the standard pay for other ministers.[38] In the more typical operations wherein proprietor and editor were the same, of course all the liabilities of ownership were suffered. Many editors received only limited compensation, therefore, and depended on the unlikely event that their papers made a profit. Many of the editors simply performed the service without any compensation at all and depended entirely on other sources of income.

Under the circumstances, leaving the pastorate for the editorial desk was often an unpleasant experience. More than the frustrations of the job and inadequate pay were painful, for nearly all of these men had originally felt an urgent obligation toward a regular ministry. "The work of a Christian minister," wrote the editor of the *Ohio Observer*, "is the work to which life has been directed from our earliest years, and we can be content in no other."[39] The editor of the *Presbyterian of the West* "would have rejoiced still to have pursued . . . the delightful, though arduous toil, of building up the church of God," as preacher "of His everlasting gospel."[40] The religious newspaper was, however, another agency of the gospel, and serving its goals was not a radical departure from the essence of the ministerial call. But it was the vision of expanded contacts with the public by way of the printed page which most often overcame repugnance for the job. When Thomas Brainard was asked to edit the *Cincinnati*

Journal he said an emphatic "no" because "he felt an extreme reluctance to assume new and oppressive responsibilities in another field of labor." It took four months of thought and the persuasion of friends to induce him to change his mind. He finally accepted the post on the basis "that every man is bound to expend his influence, where it will promote the greatest good."[41] The editor of the *Western Christian,* who also preferred the pastorate, took the job only because no one else could be found for it,[42] a factor which very often was the only inducement.

Because of these factors, the editors were inclined to be apologetic and to reflect the obvious insecurity of the stranger to this kind of work. They freely acknowledged both their mechanical and editorial blunders, pleading not only lack of time but inexperience. Sometimes a man was acutely aware that the work was beyond his intellectual capacity.[43] An Indiana Baptist ventured "forth with trembling" into the untried waters with "naturally inadequate" qualifications only to be further hampered by a serious affliction of his eyes.[44] An Episcopalian in Ohio explained his aversion to the task on the basis of inexperience, the heavy pressures of other duties, and "a real distrust of our competency to the undertaking."[45] These were expressions of genuine anguish, not of false modesty.

It was so rare for an editor to express any affection for his job as to be an exception worth reporting. Such an oddity was John Lawrence, an editor of the *Religious Telescope,* whose work was more exclusively editorial than most. He acknowledged the tendency among editors to complain, adding that, for himself, he found editing busy but not unpleasant. "If an editor is a good-natured man, industrious, has tact and a fertile mind, he will be as happy as men are generally; but if he is lazy, keeps a dirty office, smokes to excess, has a great desire for praise, an ill-temper, and a brain that must be cudgelled into activity, he will have a sorry time of it."[46] The normal response to the editorial assignment was more like that of the editor of the *Methodist Correspondent*. He published one version of a reaction which was widely circulated among editors. Provided he could find a moral means of release from his duties, he wrote, "I would wish that the task in the future might devolve on my worst enemy. I should then have the satisfaction of seeing him amply punished."[47]

A young novice editor began his career as editor of the *Cincinnati Journal* in a state of shock and years later he wrote of the experience. "I was 28 years of age only. I had never seen a newspaper made up, and of the details of editing was profoundly ignorant. I was stunned by the cry of 'copy!' 'copy!'.... I was heartily sick of myself and the whole concern for the first three or four weeks." He seemed never to have become fully reconciled to the job. "But I was on a treadmill, and must keep stepping until practice gave me some skill, and habit made my work tolerable."[48] The *Journal* ceased publication when another of its editors could no longer cope with such pressures. He could find no replacement and he was the only man left in the establishment near the end of the summer who was not sick or otherwise out of action. He gave up and took a vacation from which he never returned.[49]

Many editors complained that, while Christians could spare their pastors for a vacation, there was never any relief from the editor's task. "Whatever else is neglected, the work of the editor must be performed.—Whether the times be lively or dull, the weather hot or cold, the editor sick or well, his work must be done, and that, too, just at a certain time."[50] It added insult to injury when the brethren presumed upon the editor because he was already confined to the city to tend also the flock while the vacationing pastor replenished himself.[51]

The editorial columns teemed with references to the "onerous" nature of the editorial responsibilities and to "the prison house of unceasing toil and anxious care."[52] It is less than surprising, then, that there were dozens of references to frustrated or postponed efforts to resign the position and get relief from its burdens. The fact that more than a handful of religious newspapers were published is a remarkable tribute to editors' and owners' commitment to this agency.

In spite of his own reluctance and intense dissatisfaction with his work, the editor of a religious newspaper contributed much to his denomination. The editor, almost without exception, consciously served and appealed to a denominational constituency from one of the most sensitive and influential positions in his church. It was a part of his commission to stimulate harmony and growth in his group. This responsibility to some extent limited editorial freedom but it was rarely a galling feature. It was in the diversity of his readers in an age of passionate controversy that the editor found the greatest challenge to his freedom and integrity.

The readers of denominational newspapers may have tended to accept the articles of faith and polity of their institutions, but among these readers were diverse tastes, interests, viewpoints, and educational levels which must be satisfied by a multipurpose paper. One of the strongest features of the interior mechanism of the editor was his awareness that he must seek to please readers "whose tastes are as different as their features."[53] Many readers wanted more or less on temperance, Romanism, or slavery; some more or less of political news, market reports, or other elements of a secular nature. As conciliatory as he might be by nature, one of the editor's burdens was the knowledge of "the absolute impossibility of pleasing all his readers, and the certainty of displeasing even those who under other circumstances would be sincere and warm friends."[54]

Living "peaceably with all men" inside or outside the church might be a goal of the editor but it was difficult to attain even in the best ordered church families. It was impossible to take all sides and it was often inconsistent with the temperament of the editor to attempt to, and herein was the nature of the dilemma for many of them.[55] They must also claim the right to let their own education, tastes, feelings, or, as in one case, let the fact of youth representing a new generation in the church influence the policies of the paper.[56] The clerical editor of this generation was rarely disposed to conceive of his responsibilities in terms of surveying his readers to "discover their opinions and prejudices, and make a report to meet their desires."[57] The same sense of duty which compelled men to take up this unpleasant task would hardly permit them to ignore their own conscience in the treatment of issues. "Neutralism" or "noncommittalism . . . would add much to our awkwardness, as such policy comes very unnatural."[58]

Not only was it morally reprehensible to be neutral, but for an editor to be so would deprive the reader of an essential element in his own development. "It is by the collision of mind with mind that men's wits are sharpened, and their reasoning powers are invigorated."[59] It became, then, a goal of many editors to educate their reading public to accept the impossibility of "harmonious agreement among men," and on the other hand to accept the necessity of *"cordial agreement to differ* on many points." No paper could continue its service for long "unless our good brethren . . . have the magnanimity to adopt this principle."[60]

Issues with a political bearing were especially delicate for no editor could afford political partisanship. On political questions interpreted as having a moral bearing, however, for an editor to "hold his peace through fear of giving offense is, simply, pusillanimous. . . . It is, for a conscientious editor, a matter of real anxiety in what way to do his duty as a citizen, and as a teacher of religion and of morals in their broadest applications, without compromising his usefulness by erring toward either extreme."[61] Editors of religious newspapers were convinced that, if they avoided partisanship, they could play a role superior to that of their secular neighbors in imparting a knowledge of "the true state of public affairs."[62]

The result of this introspection was that many editors did eventually assume an explicit and partisan position on certain key issues such as slavery. In most cases the editorial policy was directed toward the center. More often than not, this position was naturally assumed by the editor. Where one did become overly partisan, it usually resulted in some form of restriction from the denomination in those cases where this form of official control existed.[63] When it did not exist, the reactions of subscribers and area leaders operated to force the more extreme out of the editorial chair. Epaphras Goodman was persuaded to sell his interest in the *Cincinnati Journal* to others who, although not pro-slavery by any means, yet realized that if the paper was to serve as an effective organ of the New School Presbyterian Church it must be more moderate in tone. Other papers whose editors attempted to focus on controversy and would not be tempered, soon succumbed.

On the other hand, an editor could be too moderate. It is entirely possible that Charles Elliott lost enough support that he was voted out of his post with the *Western Christian Advocate*[64] by the General Conference in 1856 because his position on a radical proposal to exclude all lay slaveholders from membership in the Methodist Church was not strong enough. Elliott had been firmly opposed to slavery, had supported the northern Church vigorously in the division in 1844, had been assigned to write the northern view of the history of that division, and had written extensively otherwise in opposition to slavery. Yet he refused to say that all slaveholders were sinful or to support editorially the change of rule. Later, he became the editor of the *Central Christian Advocate* in St. Louis, probably because his moderation was an asset where the strategy of the Church in slave territory made it appropriate.

The net effect of the religious newspaper was to develop and support a denominational consensus. The editor's self-discipline and his exercise of discipline over correspondents accrued to the benefit of conciliation and accommodation within the church. This policy produced a more tolerant spirit in handling internal controversy. Many editors felt that they had seen progress along this line during their tenure, a development which had made editorial work more pleasant. "Brethren can now express their views on subjects on which there are different opinions," one wrote, "without getting into an endless controversy."[65]

The denomination was only one corner of the editor's parish. The editor of a typical religious newspaper included in his mission the world beyond the parochial boundary. The religious newspaper was a unique instrument of the churches' impingement upon the world of God and man. One of the most obvious features of that world in the United States during the first half of the nineteenth century was an unparalleled and rapidly expanding diversity of religious faith and practice.

Chapter III
COPING WITH RELIGIOUS DIVERSITY

The religious development of the Old Northwest to 1861 involved all the diversity characteristic of the United States generally, plus some of its own. The major denominations were present in their full vigor, accenting differences of doctrine and polity and competing with each other for influence. The Northwest was also a setting for the expansion of every active religious minority in America, including the Roman Catholics, Jews, Mormons, Universalists, Millerites, and Spiritualists. In the age of the common man, this free enterprise system in religion represented one of the values inherent in the cultivation of individual preference. There was also a vast area of potential controversy over definite and substantial differences in doctrine, polity, and views of the churches' role in society.

With all the diversity, there was enough emphasis on church union in that generation to give editors a point for fixing their definition of Christian unity. There were many endeavors in which denominational lines were either crossed or ignored. Among these were home missionary work, the printing and distribution of religious literature, the promotion of Sunday Schools, and certain types of reform such as temperance. These early ecumenical activities probably grew more out of weakness than conviction. Most editors supported such united efforts only until their own denominations became self-sufficient in those fields.

There was also an international union movement, the Evangelical Alliance, which culminated in a meeting in London in 1846. Some of those associated with religious newspapers in the West attended. The purpose of the Alliance was to promote union in behalf of such abstract goals as increasing the effectiveness of Christian activity, advancing religious freedom, and generally promoting the gospel. There was some American initiative in this movement, but any effective promotion of a branch of the Alliance in the United States was interrupted by the Civil War.[1]

Men of all persuasions limited their definition of fraternity to "brotherly friendship," "a liberal and kind spirit toward others," "love and meekness," a common emphasis on the "fundamentals of the gospel," or mingling pleasantly with others at nonchurch functions. Such phrases as these were generally qualified by editors in order to make it clear that they did not intend "amalgamation," that they felt they must "act on their own views," and that they must not regard "error with as much complacency as truth."[2]

Although many churchmen searched very cautiously for the meaning of unity through charity and tolerance, a few editors were pugnacious, showing lapses of both temper and taste. The editor of a very short-lived paper called the *Olive Branch* came out with the symbol of peace in one hand and the sword in the other "to wage a successful war with infidels, atheists, sceptics, drunkards, and manstealers, Unitarians, Universalists and Pantheists, self-righteous Pharisees, nominal christians and worldlings."[3] An Old School Presbyterian would have none of the "spurious" charity which would temper his opposition to "Papists, Unitarians, Universalists, Campbellites, Swedenborgians, Dunkers, New Lights, Socinians, Infidels, or Atheists."[4] One pair of prominent editors found a unique and rather harmless way of demeaning each other. The editor of the *Religious Telescope* chastised the editor of the *Western Christian Advocate* by printing his name without using capital letters. The editor of the *Advocate* then professed to be returning good for evil by wishing "for the editor of the telescope more grace and more sense."[5]

Several editors developed some interesting refinements in referring to a contemporary as an ass. The editor of the *Protestant Monitor* was direct about it when a brother minister began a competing paper in the Illinois Conference of the Methodist Protestant Church.[6] In another case, when a northern Methodist editor advertised for a man to work in his office, a southern Methodist replied that indeed the office was in need of a man. The response was: "But, Dr., if we had wanted a fully-developed pair of ears and a gigantic braying apparatus, we should have lost no time in advertising, but have sent at once to the office of the *St. Louis Advocate*. The article is there, in good condition, only needing currying."[7] This kind of personal invective, although rare, was indeed a part of the panorama of religious journalism in the Northwest.

The most challenging gap in understanding involved Catholics and Protestants. Controversy between them had an historical base in Europe quite independent of any immediate occasion or emotion. In America, the historical and hardly latent animosities were intensified inevitably with the migration of German and Irish Catholics before the Civil War. The disparity of religious views, the quantity of immigrants with these views, and economic and social competition all contributed to the political and religious crusades against aliens and Catholics. The controversy was a continuous theme in Protestant literature, but its intensification coincided with the first major proliferation of religious newspapers in Ohio just before 1830.

Reactions in the Northwest paralleled reactions drawn largely from the East and presented in Ray Allen Billington's *Protestant Crusade, 1800—1860*. His treatment of the West was primarily from the perspective of the churches and their agencies in the East. He cited sources which were intended to show that there was little interest in Catholicism among western missionaries through 1840 except, perhaps, as an emphasis useful in inducing alarmed easterners to give financial support to missions.[8] This alleged indifference did not apply to the numerous editors and proprietors of religious newspapers in the West. Their early reactions to Catholicism were inspired by the same historical animosity that affected eastern Protestants and by the increasing presence of Roman Catholic immigrants in the West.

The West had its own Catholic element as early as the 1820's and 1830's, and a very considerable indigenous, nativistic, anti-Catholic movement developed in reaction to it. The Detroit area had 2,000 Catholics as early as 1815.[9] One of Cincinnati's eleven churches in 1819 was Catholic and two of sixteen were by 1840. There were 5,000 German Catholics in and near Cincinnati in 1834.[10] New dioceses were established in Cincinnati in 1823, in St. Louis in 1826, and in Detroit in 1832.[11] In 1831 the Catholics created their own newspaper, the *Catholic Telegraph,* in Cincinnati. All of the original antagonism between Catholics and Protestants, combined with their concentration together in such places as Cincinnati, produced continuous attack and rebuttal in the press. Catholic and Protestant editors were equally intemperate in ridiculing the most sacred beliefs, practices, and heroes of the other's faith.

The first paper in the region to sound a warning against Catholic encroachment in the West was the Plan of Union *Western Intelligencer* in an editorial titled, "A Loud Call to Protestants." An invasion force of twenty-one Catholic priests supported by a Papal appropriation of $100,000 had landed in the East, their destination the Mississippi Valley. "Let Christians and patriots lie still, until Popery has gained an ascendancy—until it shall prevail, and it will ask no more. Fire and sword and the Inquisition will do the rest." The *Cincinnati Journal* soon repeated the alarm. The aims of the Catholic Church, the editor warned, had not changed since the Dark Ages. Only its "crooked and variant policies" had changed. The Catholics would seem to flow with the currents of popular democracy after which they would execute deep and well-laid plans to conquer America by force of numbers and through the propaganda distributed to the unsuspecting Protestant children in Catholic schools. "We do not intend by these remarks to preach up a crusade against the Catholics. But we do think it is time that a reasonable alarm should be excited,"[12] wrote the editor.

The *Catholic Telegraph* came into being mainly to answer such charges and the Catholics were thereafter ably and aggressively defended.[13] One of the most dangerous elements in Protestantism according to James Mullon, its first editor, was "an undisciplined perusal of the Scriptures" which gave rise often to "delusive theories of promoting the happiness of the human race." The editor was prompted to ask: "Can we seriously imagine, that a book so comprehensive in its matter, so elliptical in its language, and so dark in its mysteries, was ever intended to be the sole guide of the bulk of mankind, who, notwithstanding every effort, must be ignorant, from the necessity of their condition?"[14] However able this argument, its intellectually aristocratic and authoritarian tone indicated the profoundly real gap between the Catholics and the Protestants in the Northwest in the age of the common man.

Mullon ridiculed the Protestant missionary and benevolent institutions, dismissing all of them as crassly selfish means for some individuals to get money at the expense of others. Missionaries were "supported in a life of luxurious ease." He accused them of selling the clothing sent to the Mackinaw Mission and pocketing the money. The efforts of female missionaries there to get materials and utensils with which to make clothing were dismissed as "indelicate beggary." The enormous sums of money spent in "transporting and maintaining the Rev. Instruments *male* and *female*" and "piously filched from honest members of society" would be the most remembered features of their enterprise.[15] The *Telegraph* labeled the revival the masterpiece "of all the trickery, that has ever been practised on the credulity of the multitude." The revivalist used revolting stories, with women and girls especially tending to lose their equilibrium under these "artifices." Revivals were "a scandal to religion; a mockery on common sense, mere trickery to cheat the understanding and keep up the delusion; by which the *knowing* ones may maintain the cause by which they eat and drink."[16]

Mullon, a convert to Catholicism as a surprisingly large number of Catholic editors were, resisted the efforts of some to temper his attacks. Some insisted that the unfounded charges of Protestants should be ignored. He refused to accept this counsel during his tenure and in 1834 Bishop John Purcell took over the editorial page. Under the Bishop, and, after 1839, under his brother, Edward Purcell, the attacks and counterattacks by the *Telegraph* depended for their effectiveness more upon reason than upon invective.

By the mid-1830's, all major religious newspapers were taking notice of the increased Catholic immigration into the Northwest. These immigrants were "*totally unlike* the original inhabitants of these States."[17] They were "neither as intelligent nor as moral as the Protestants" of previous migrations. At the peak of such interest, news came to Cincinnati of the burning of the Ursuline Convent in Charlestown, Massachusetts, August 11, 1834. A very complex background of "class antipathies, religious jealousies, and economic conditions" plus intense agitation against the Catholics from the Protestant pulpit and press in the Boston area produced the mob of primarily lower-class people who attacked and burned the Convent. The immediate cause of the furor was the circulation of rumors relating to Elizabeth Harrison, a member of the order who collapsed emotionally under her teaching duties and quite innocently left the convent, returning the next day. This incident was distorted by Protestants into a forced return and imprisonment by Catholic authorities.[18]

There was a brief moment when both Protestant and Catholic editors in the Northwest seemed stunned into silence by these appalling results from unbridled tongues and pens. They soon recovered their equilibrium and began to place the incident in typically partisan perspective. Protestants denounced the mob's actions as outrageous, but perpetrators of the outrage were denounced as much because their methods were self-defeating as that they originated "in folly and wickedness."[19] Most of the blame was placed on the Catholics. The mob was ignorant of the facts about Miss Harrison because the Catholics had not released adequate information. "The rabble did not know whether the *nun* was dead or alive, whether she was free or in chains. And it was this suspense, the ignorance of the true state of the case, which led the misguided beings to their fearful and guilty work."[20]

The editor of the *Telegraph* pointed to the triumph of magnanimity in a bishop's sermon in the Boston area, on forgiveness in the midst of "the masked faces and the assumed disguise of cold-blooded and preconcerted villainy." He expected the incident to arouse the indignation of "the intelligent and virtuous" against those upon whom the responsibility rested, "the *inhuman Editors* who pander to the ferocious passions of the mob."[21]

Soon after this episode several highly successful books appeared which claimed to expose life in the convent from the perspective of former residents. The most prominent of the books was Maria Monk's *Awful Disclosures of the Hotel Dieu Nunnery of Montreal,* first published in 1836, with a sequel in 1837. More than 300,000 copies of her books sold before the Civil War. Maria Monk, by her own mother's account, had never been in Hotel Dieu but she had gone to a Catholic Magdalen establishment to bear one of her illegitimate children. She was crudely and fraudulently exploited by the commercial press and anti-Catholic charlatans. The substance of her book consisted of the account of the access nuns and priests had to each other for sexual purposes and the infanticide practiced to cover the results. Two Protestant clergymen subsequently inspected the interior of Hotel Dieu and reported that it was completely different from the structural details given in Maria's *Disclosures*. William L. Stone, editor of the *Commercial Advertiser* in New York and a Protestant, also made a thorough inspection and left convinced that the book was utterly false.[22]

Some Protestant editors showed concern over the public display of the "brothel details with which priests and nuns are conversant." The Methodist editor in Cincinnati fully believed Miss Monk's revelations, but he advised Protestants to stop supporting the publication of these indelicate matters, discussion of which was scripturally forbidden, whether true or not.[23] Most Protestant editors did feel that the *Disclosures* and other books like it were credible because they fitted the widely circulated gossip over what existed among the male and female orders of the Catholic Church. Many, therefore, accepted the *Disclosures* as authentic and refused to change their minds even after the results of the impartial investigations were published. A United Brethren editor believed that Stone had been deceived by clever alterations in the walls and rooms of Hotel Dieu which he could not detect because of the hurried nature of his "guided" tour "performed in the amazing short space of a few hours." The Methodist paper dismissed the investigators as chosen friends of the priests and dismissed the Jesuits as such liars that their affidavits were worthless.[24]

The new finesse of the *Catholic Telegraph* appeared dramatically in Bishop Purcell's reaction to Maria Monk whom he believed to be the victim of unscrupulous clergymen, her own lust, and her own delusions. He was convinced that the Protestants had fallen into a trap of their own making. After Miss Monk had disappeared temporarily, he pleaded, "But, gentlemen, we beg, we entreat you, not to charge us with the abduction of

Maria; she belongs not to us—we do not dispute your right to her; her book is yours—herself is yours; she is indebted to you for her reputation—she is one of your 'immediate jewels.'... Keep her, gentlemen, keep her; as her book is driven from decent society, she will serve to remind you that such a *thing* was written." The Presbyterian clergy, he contended, had "fallen so low, that men publicly declared, that they will take good care how they permit a clergyman, zealous for Maria Monk and her book, to associate with the females of their families!"[25]

The Protestant editors were not so gullible later in the presence of the small army of men who posed as former priests and became professional, anti-Catholic lecturers. Evidently Allessandro Gavazzi was the most compelling and the best received in the Northwest. The editor of the *Religious Telescope,* however, was one who rejected him and his "spiteful denunciations" in favor of the "revival and progress of VITAL GODLINESS—A PURE AND PRACTICAL CHRISTIANITY."[26] "Father" Leahy, who was finally sentenced to life in prison for killing a man, and L. Giustiniani, who travelled with a group of Germans whom he "converted" at each stop,[27] found little support among western clergy. There were objections to their use of "obscenities" before mixed audiences, their tendency to lie about the number of their converts, and the charging of an admission to the lectures as "a novel mode of exposing *Priestcraft*."[28] Yet another indication that there were limits to the appeal of the more concentrated and violent expressions of anti-Catholic sentiment was the fact that all religious newspapers established as anti-Catholic organs in the Northwest failed quickly.[29]

Local political confrontation between Catholics and Protestants in Ohio involved the schools. The Catholic schools in Cincinnati were enrolling 2,607 pupils in 1848, including some Protestant children. A number of issues, including Bible reading in the public schools, compulsory school attendance laws, and funds for school libraries, came to focus in the spring election of 1853.[30] The staff of the *Telegraph* unwisely threatened the politicians with the wrath of 200,000 Catholics at the polls should the school bill pass. "We promise before hand to those who vote for it, all the political hostility which can combine against them."[31]

The *Telegraph* had previously carefully established its platform on public schools. Education had to be based on religion or it would be a curse. The Church must control education and like "a fond mother" repel efforts to estrange her children. Public schools obviously did not, as claimed by Protestants, induce virtue in the population in view of the daily record of increasing crime. It was absolutely necessary "that each member of society know what *he ought* to do and be furnished with a powerful motive for doing it." Only authoritarian education within the context of the true faith could establish this moral authority and preserve republican institutions. Instead of being democratic as claimed, the public school system was a "monstrous despotism," embodying the notion that children were the property of the state.[32]

Protestant editors found their worst fears confirmed in these declarations. The Protestant press in the Northwest was almost unanimous in its fervent support of the common schools and had been for many years. Conversely, they opposed parochial schools on the stated grounds that they would destroy the public schools or weaken their moral influence, that they would promote division in American society, and that they would threaten democracy by leaving the majority uneducated.[33]

The Protestant point of view triumphed in the election. The editor of the Methodist *Advocate* headlined his post-election editorial, "Defeat of the Pope in Cincinnati." He warned of the necessity for further vigilance against the "foreign religious and political power," in order "that they may not overthrow our liberties.'' Even the editor of the Universalist *Star,* sometimes sympathetic with Catholics against orthodox Protestants, expressed his joy.[34] The editor of the *Telegraph* reacted bitterly to the results. He believed, however, that in spite of a triumph for ''insane bigotry,'' there had been some beneficial effects. Some ''native American Catholics, particularly the young men'' who ''were fascinated with what are called liberal opinions'' and who had not known the oppression endured by Catholics elsewhere ''had in mind a beautiful theory of toleration which they thought was identical with republicanism.... Well, they have been cured with a vengeance! They know all about Protestantism now!—''[35]

Protestant editors continued into the 1850's to express concern over the influx of foreigners, particularly the Catholic Irish and both Catholic and rationalist Germans. They had always been confident, however, that Protestant doctrines and institutions and those of the Republic were sufficiently powerful to absorb this tide without injury.[36] It was difficult for Protestant editors to accept the curtailment of immigration advocated by the Know Nothings, for it would be working against the Providence which had sent refugees to America from the poverty and oppression of Europe.[37] Many also stated the view that foreigners contributed to the nation's wealth. Both church and state, it was commonly felt, should rejoice in the opportunity to elevate and convert them.[38] But in conflict with these positive attitudes there was a growing concern over the political potential of the Catholic masses as papers widely reported that politicians were openly courting Catholic voters in various parts of the Northwest.[39]

The Know Nothing movement attempted to translate this fear into a political party with rather mixed results in the Northwest. The movement's greatest success was probably in the vicinity of Cincinnati and in central and southern Illinois. There was much use of the anti-Catholic theme in some of the leading secular papers of

Cincinnati, and there were several Know Nothing papers started in the area. Elsewhere in the Northwest, the Know Nothing movement had shallow roots, serving as an instrument for people who had not quite found a home in the confused political climate of the decade. The anti-Nebraska party, soon to be the Republican party, was destined to become the political home of the majority.[40]

The reactions to Know Nothingism in the Protestant press were quite mixed. Open endorsement of the Know Nothings was unusual but the two Methodist editors in the Northwest showed so much interest in the movement that they inspired considerable reaction in the Democratic press. Elliott in Cincinnati blamed the Catholics' desire for political control and secrecy of method for the rise of the Know Nothings with their secrecy, which he approved as an unavoidable feature of the war against the Catholics. He anticipated much good from the party even though he did not belong to it and even though he mildly disapproved of its exclusion of foreign-born Protestants from membership. Elliott also mentioned and approved numerous Know Nothing newspapers appearing in the area and elsewhere. There were some significant qualifications, however, in his support, which indicated that the party did not have a blank check. He hoped that the Know Nothings would avoid extremes on other issues so that they might be more effective with the one narrow principle of opposition to Popish, political influence. Those bidding for office must also be men of proved ability and character. It was not safe to follow someone simply because of his stand on this one issue.[41]

Elliott grew suspicious of the motives of the Know Nothings and he found a case in point in Cincinnati. The Superintendent of the Cincinnati Court House advertised for laborers and mechanics to work on a new building with preference to be given to American Protestants. "This is quite another matter," wrote Elliott, "from restraining and opposing foreign political influence, by regulating naturalization laws." Restricting the employment of "Romanists" as workers was not only unnecessary but "unjust in itself."[42]

Watson, Elliott's colleague in Chicago, saw in the Know Nothing movement the opportunity to oppose Catholics' political power without trespassing on their right to follow their own religious practices. He was willing to endure the defects of the Know Nothings "until the last nunnery, convent, or secret cell of imprisoned females, shall either be suppressed by law or by the power that razed the Ursuline Convent within sight of the Bunker-hill [sic] monument."[43]

Most Protestants were more reserved in approval of the Know Nothings than these two Methodists. Secrecy was antirepublican, the exclusion of immigrants from politics denied them a natural right, and there was a suspicion of the use of methods other than moral suasion to accomplish Know Nothing goals. The most important influence on editors in their rejection of Know Nothingism was in the party's tendency to defend slavery, or at least to waver on that issue.[44] This issue also kept the Methodist editors from any final commitment to the party as such.

The foreign-language segment of the religious press had its unique variety of Americanism. The Scandinavian newspapers, as did the foreign-language press generally, encouraged Americanization by urging the immigrant to use the English language and the public schools. They carefully explained the Know Nothing movement to their readers, then understandably rejected it. It was found to be anti-immigrant, anti-Catholic, and anti-American while hypocritically masquerading as pro-American. A Swedish editor did sympathize with the Know Nothing reaction to the Irish Catholics and the radical Germans, but he refused to sanction Know Nothing secrecy. He deemed the party a positive threat to American liberties.[45]

The *Catholic Telegraph* was more restrained during the early and middle fifties than it had been before. Perhaps the key to the editor's attitude was the view that the times were so "excited" that it was not possible to counter the lies in circulation. He also found some danger himself from the radical Germans, *"in their capacity as foreigners."* He even saw elements of a British conspiracy in the Know Nothing party which might be subdued by a large influx of Americans into the order. The editor asked for an understanding of the bigots as *"men* working under the influence of human passions, prejudices, interests—such as might, without the grace of God, subject any one of us." Bigots would eventually help spread the truth because of the obvious contradictions among them and because constant controversy would stimulate reason. The editor predicted that one day the American people would "look upon the page that tells of the present illiberal treatment of Catholics in this country as another foul blot, in addition to those of the Blue Laws of Connecticut, the burning of witches, the boring of ears of Quakers, and the persecution and exile of Roger Williams."[46]

The *Telegraph* counseled Catholic voters to approach cautiously the fall election in Cincinnati in 1854. Catholics should be models of propriety and be sure that they met all technical requirements for voting. After the defeat in the election of all area Democrats who had been effectively slandered by the Know Nothings, the editor warned the people of Cincinnati that the growth of the city and its prosperity rested on immigration and a general liberality of sentiment. If bigotry successfully asserted itself, the city's resources would dry up.[47]

The Jew and his faith were very rarely the object of attack in the Northwest in this era. The thinness of the Jewish population in the upper Mississippi Valley and in America generally, undoubtedly had something to do with that fact. It was 1836 before Cincinnati had a synagogue and only eight cities in Ohio had congregations by 1860. The few Jews in the Northwest also lacked the cohesiveness of other groups outside the prevailing orthodoxy.[48] Christian editors had always shown an interest in Judaism as a historical part of their own religion. When confronted with the Jews as a small entity in the population of the United States, therefore, there was a tendency to react benignly except for urging proselytizing among them.[49]

Wise, as editor of the *Israelite* and *Deborah*, was able, therefore, to devote relatively more time to the reform of Judaism than he did to a defense of Jews against Gentiles. He gave much attention to political movements in Europe which tended toward more or less liberalization for the Jews but nearly always in a context of appreciation for the favorable condition of Jews in America. He was initially both naïve and revealing of his own bias in his reactions to the Know Nothings. He attributed the anti-Catholic mood to "the arrogance of some Catholic bishops." When not threatened by Catholic power "the American people is a liberal, noble-minded, unprejudiced, charitable, and tolerant nation." Americans were too practical to let the prejudice within their churches carry over into business. Even the "old habits and prejudices" of the Irish and German immigrants might be overcome after they saw how the Jew was received by native Americans.[50] Wise was not indifferent to the anti-Jewish aspect of Christian doctrine, and the implications of campaigns to convert the Jews to Christianity. Most of the infrequent references to Jews in Christian papers were concerned with the conversion of the Jew as a fulfillment of prophecy. It was a specialty of German-oriented groups to speculate about this and to propose the means of proselytizing.[51] Wise reacted to these efforts at three points: he doubted the successes claimed for missionaries abroad, he declared that no Jew would be converted to a system that had so much difficulty in locating which religion of Jesus was the proper one, and he denied that Jews ever crucified a person named Jesus.[52]

It soon became clear that Wise had revised his original optimism about Americans. Religious liberty might be just as insecure in the hands of Protestants as in the hands of Catholics. The combination of religion with politics was especially "disgusting." The Know Nothing reaction to the minority of Catholics was an absurdity. "Do not," he wrote, "so badly slander and outrage republicanism, as to tell us the lowest and most despicable passions... of religious fanaticism and intolerance are necessary to guard republicanism." Wise believed that the Know Nothings were opposed to all foreigners and all creeds except the Protestant; hence Jews were ultimately vulnerable before them.[53]

Wise eventually became bitterly disillusioned with "Illiberality in the United States." He denounced Sunday laws, chastised Christian ministers as "petty Jesuits," and ranged abroad to denounce Massachusetts for adding a "Christian" requirement for office. The occasion for his wrath was that "here [in Cincinnati] a parcel of aldermen, ruled by priests and women, impose on us a Sunday law," an outrage which only slaves would bear. He scorned the people who grieved for the suffering slave and "so furiously for bleeding Kansas" and yet passed this kind of law.[54]

The most sordid exchanges between orthodox Protestants and other groups, exclusive of the Catholics, were with the Universalists. There were, of course, interminable arguments over the doctrine of eternal punishment based on reason and partisan interpretations of the Bible. The Universalist was a debater, not an evangelist, and he was a very aggressive challenger whether in the press or on the platform. He was high on the list of those beyond the range of tolerance among the orthodox. Orthodox editors found various indications of immoral tendencies among the Universalists and thought that the attractive-

ness of these pernicious tendencies among the uncon-
verted might well have accounted for their growth.[55]
Murders, insanity, and suicides[56] were often the products
of Universalism since the restraints of hell fire were
needed to keep people moral and normal.[57] One editor
charged that "all the filth of society follow after Universalism.... You make the people of the city of Chicago
believe that Universalism is true, and it would not be safe
for a woman to walk in the streets; it would be a complete brothel."[58]

Universalists were adept at reversing these charges. All
kinds of crimes and mental illnesses emanated from the
"partialist" doctrine of endless hell. And no less than
eleven "limitarian" clergymen were confined to the
penitentiary at Auburn, New York. The *Star* passed on
the news "that a flaming preacher has just been turned
out of the church for having more children than his
share." The ultimate scoop and sweet revenge involved
two Methodist preachers who had recently claimed that a
certain Universalist had recanted on his deathbed. The
two were later tried "for the besetting sin of too many of
that class of people ... being too intimate with certain
sisters."[59] As in the Catholic press at one time, Universalists reduced all benevolent enterprises of the Protestants to craven begging. Tract peddling was one of several conspiracies against the rights of the people as the
orthodox intruded "these dirty little things into families"
where they were not wanted. The structure of the
Methodist Church allowed for oppression and tyranny
and the people were "the mere tools of their spiritual
guides"; hence, the Methodist Church was a threat to the
civil liberties of all citizens of the United States.[60]

The Universalists and the orthodox repeatedly challenged each other's claims of success in gaining converts
from the opponent's faith. This issue was quicksand for
any faction since there was considerable religious mobility both horizontally and vertically in those days. Some-

times a convert would be claimed, highly publicized, then revert to his original faith or even to something entirely different.[61]

Mormonism, while an American product, constituted a very special problem in religious understanding. It was born of young Joseph Smith's unusual conversion in 1820 in Palmyra, New York, and of his extraordinary claims to special revelations by way of the famous gold plates. The Mormons moved from Palmyra to Kirtland on the Western Reserve in the early 1830's. A colony was then established in Missouri where Smith eventually went, but intense conflict resulted in flight to Illinois. The Mormon establishment itself split over polygamy and eventually serious conflict once more developed with the authority of the state. A mob murdered Joseph and his brother, Hyrum, June 27, 1844, while they were being held in the Carthage jail. The Old Northwest, then, was the principal stage for the first generation of Mormon development before the dispersion and the famous trek to Utah.[62]

It could be taken for granted that Mormon claims to unique revelation, their colonization and isolation, and their own belligerence in repeated confrontations with other citizens and public authorities would invite unfavorable attention. Mormon leaders were "hypocrites" and full of "blasphemous pretensions" was the judgement of a Presbyterian. They were foolish and impious and offensive to the welfare of society, charged an Episcopalian. A United Brethren editor suggested that in religious matters the Mormons might be "idiots." A Universalist agreed with the orthodox in holding that Mormonism was "one of the most miserable humbugs in existence."[63]

The persecution of the Mormons and the violence perpetrated against them nevertheless evoked sympathy. There was a tendency, as in the case of Catholics, both to condemn the violence and to charge the Mormons themselves with courting retribution.[64] When troubles developed for the Mormons in Missouri, however, a

United Brethren editor believed that they had "been more sinned against than sinning." Whatever the origins of Mormon troubles he wished the state well in punishing the persecutors.[65] When the Smiths were murdered, editors of all persuasions and from all parts of the Northwest seemed genuinely shocked and outraged. They refused to accept press versions which found extenuating circumstances for the guilty parties or that the Smiths had acted in other than good faith with local authorities. Editors from within and without the state of Illinois harshly condemned state authorities for what they interpreted as inaction.[66] On the other hand, the religious press uniformly supported the government in its conflict with the Mormons in Utah during the "Mormon War," sanctioning such use of force as was necessary.[67] This element also encouraged Congressional action against the greatest distraction of all, polygamy. The practice placed the Constitution in jeopardy and even though it was enclosed within the framework of religious faith, it could not be allowed. If it required a constitutional amendment to destroy polygamy, so be it.[68]

Most groups found it more difficult to define a position on the teaching of William Miller than on the other deviations within Protestantism. Miller was another product of the revival who became increasingly obsessed with the Second Advent of Christ which he finally calculated would occur in March, 1843. The problem for evangelical preachers and editors was that millenial theology and adventist teachings were a part of their own heritage. They could not dismiss lightly either Miller's teachings or the substantial inroads he made on their congregations. Most, however, emphatically rejected Miller's forecast of a specific date for the Second Advent on both practical and scriptural grounds. There was evident regional pride in the fact that Millerism had not stirred the Northwest as it had the East. It bothered the chauvinistic westerner that easterners thought them more unstable and more

63

susceptible to excitement and error. Any system of error "will find more followers, out of any given number of inhabitants, in New England, than it will in the western states,"[69] declared an Ohio Baptist, in rebuttal. There was, nevertheless, concern among the orthodox that the failure of Miller's predictions would discredit the entire doctrine of the Second Coming of Christ or even the belief in revelation itself. Too much Millerism might also reduce or paralyze the Christian effort to convert and reform the world. Another danger was that Miller's show of great confidence in his own predictions might deceive the less sophisticated who were not well informed on Biblical chronology.[70]

Universalists met Millerism with mockery. One thought it rather foolish of Miller to have built a stone bench when only three years remained for its use. When the world did not burn in 1843, another suggested that it might be due to recent rains. The same editor came from a Millerite meeting to report that the "motley crew" must have come out of a lunatic asylum. In this he found the usual opening for an attack on "partialism," Millerism clearly being the "legitimate offspring of that doctrine." Catholics also exploited this opening. Millerism manifested the insecurity of the Protestant faith, "an indication of doubt, uncertainty and visionary expectations."[71]

The Millerites were not defenseless. After the Second Advent failed to materialize early in 1843, Joshua V. Hines, Miller's publisher and manager, brought forth the *Western Midnight Cry* in Cincinnati. The editor enjoyed the "mortification" of Methodists over the loss of some of their most valued members and local preachers.[72] A later editor had to cope with mockery in high places and did so with deadly seriousness. Some witty member of the Ohio legislature claimed to have received a petition to the end that Millerism be postponed until 1860 because the petitioners wanted to die under a Whig administration. The editor referred the petitioners to Revelations

6:16,17 which recorded the request of certain offenders that the rocks fall upon them to spare them an even worse fate at the hands of God.[73]

One more addition to America's religious diversity came from the "spirit rappings" from the toe joints of the Fox sisters in Hydeville, New York in 1848, out of which sprang the phenomenon of Spiritualism.[74] Evangelical Protestantism in this generation was, in spite of its own emotionalism, quite rationalistic in the sense that it kept its supernaturalism within closely reasoned and traditional doctrinal systems. Consequently, orthodox Protestantism was not responsive to such mystical or pseudoscientific phenomena as mesmerism, clairvoyance, phrenology, or spirit rappings. Obviously the Spiritualists found some recruits among the evangelical denominations but they found many more among the pseudo-intellectuals, educators, politicians, and those of esoteric faiths either never in, or previously drawn out of, the evangelical community. Nevertheless, the orthodox took the phenomenon seriously because so many Americans seemed susceptible to each new "pretension" which arose and because it caused mental distress among some of their own parishioners.[75] The Universalists were much more susceptible to all expressions of the occult, mystical, or mysterious in spite of Universalism's reputation as the thinking man's religion.[76]

Wise of the *Israelite* completely rejected the notion that there was any reality to the claims of Spiritualism. Spiritualism contradicted science, philosophy, and Moses. It had appeared because both Catholic and Protestant theology needed drastic reform. Protestantism with its "transcendental idealism" begat materialism and authoritarian Catholicism begat atheism. He decided that Spiritualism was largely an attempt to reconcile Protestant idealism with materialism.[77]

The editors of religious newspapers had attempted to police the domestic faith of Americans and they had thought to protect against the threat of alien faiths. If the object had been to reduce diversity in American religion or to restrain the growth of the more alien forms, they had failed. The Catholic Church had not only retained but had increased effective control over the religious life of the Catholic immigrant and was growing more rapidly than any religious group in the United States. Other immigrant groups had also managed to maintain their religious traditions and to preside over their own Americanization in spite of energetic efforts to convert them. The religious press had, for the most part, managed to reinforce rather than to weaken denominational boundaries so that religious diversity was just as characteristic as ever, if not actually increasing.

The editor of the religious paper did not stop with the effort to police the frontiers of his own or others' faith. He must also police the morals and customs of his generation. His parish extended into the world of affairs and his gospel mandate included the responsibility of telling his contemporaries how they ought to behave, a responsibility which he often seemed to relish.

Chapter IV
MORALS AND MANNERS

The religious newspapers offer an unparalleled opportunity to examine the social views held by some of the most influential figures in the churches of the Northwest. The papers themselves were a unique blend of the secular and the religious, with their editors reacting weekly to current events and issues. The church population of the region was heavily infused with revivalism and pietism from both native and Old World sources, impelling them to seek diligently to improve morals. There was a closely related revival of the gospel of work on the frontier,[1] and the vision of progress was nowhere keener than in the Northwest.[2]

The social creed for the majority of Protestants required the reform of individual behavior, social relations, institutions, cultural media, and public policy on all questions remotely considered to have a moral bearing. Churchmen were confident that they had the instruments in hand to effect reform. The church and public worship "may be regarded as the great spiritual hospital of the world, where all kinds of moral diseases ... are cured."[3] It was even a reproach upon the church that outside agencies had to be formed "to do the very work for which Christ instituted His Church."[4] The greatest possible source of strength for reformers was in the fact that *"their God is the great* Reformer of the Universe," although it required the organized church to concentrate all the "little rills of influence" into a mighty torrent.[5] Of course, the religious newspaper itself was one of the foremost agencies of improvement, and practically every editor assigned himself in some degree the mission of providing information and inspiration to that end.

Several editors were so zealous to improve public and private morality that they placed their lives and property in jeopardy. Only one man among them, Elijah Lovejoy, lost his life as a result. He attributed his unpopularity in the St. Louis area equally to his criticism of Catholics, distillers, and slaveholders. Lovejoy, ironically, was among those who condemned the indiscriminate zeal of reformers who often destroy the good in society along with the evil.[6] An irate resident of the Western Reserve personally destroyed the press of the *Ohio Observer* with a sledgehammer after its editor had charged him with adultery, concealing his name only behind initials.[7] The brother of a suicide physically attacked Amos Blanchard who had editorialized thus in the *Cincinnati Journal:* "Here is another victim to the monster dissipation and fashionable vice. We disclaim all intention of injuring the feelings of the relatives of the deceased; but we do feel constrained to warn the living, against a course whose end is temporal and eternal ruin." Blanchard simply wrestled the angry young man down and restrained him without dealing any blows himself. He expressed pity and offered his forgiveness to the family but, since he construed this as an attack on the freedom of the press, he placed the matter in the hands of the grand jury.[8]

There was little place among men of this disposition for activities or conversation, the sole purpose of which was to amuse. The case of the editor of the *Religious Telescope* might have been somewhat extreme, but it was typical of the serious tone set for the truly religious life. He was pleased to note that the preachers of the Scioto Conference showed signs of abandoning "the *sin* of jesting." It could hardly be expected that the Presbyterian who attacked the "April Fool" custom would find much place for amusement of either a public or a private character. "Lying is always sinful," he wrote. "We know of no power outside of the Church of Rome, nor indeed inside of it that can authorize anyone to tell falsehoods with impunity, even on the first day of April."[9] A Methodist made it clear that the purpose of recreation was "to fit us for business, not to be itself a business."

Even so, one should never become too earnest about it. Even the Catholics were affected by the pietism of the age. The maiming of a little girl by a firecracker, a doctor killed by a boy's play with a pistol, a bride's neck broken by a fall during a charivari, and the malignant messages conveyed by valentines under the cloak of humor raised a question as to whether amusement paid for the potential tragedy, according to the *Catholic Telegraph*.[10]

The *Israelite* alone among religious papers deliberately and uninhibitedly challenged the prevailing reactions to amusement. True religion should not, in Wise's judgment, "deprive man of innocent pleasures and amusements," but should qualify "him to distinguish true from false recreations." He thought people should be happy and sociable and that they should be encouraged to dance and to party as a means of achieving pleasure. He believed that the common position of Christians on these matters degraded the quality of true religion even while the churches failed in the weightier matters of charity and justice.[11]

Dancing was among those amusements most often denounced among orthodox Protestants, with Catholics and Universalists occasionally mildly echoing the hostility.[12] Editors consistently attempted to frighten their younger readers away from the dance by stories of sudden death, especially among the fair sex, which resulted from the physical exertions that dancing required.[13] Protestants were particularly hostile toward the inaugural balls in Washington.[14]

From an early time the circus plagued the guardians of virtue in the Old Northwest. This institution in a primitive form had made its way westward and by 1830 even remote regions were being visited by the circus with its parades, clowns, and animal exhibits.[15] A Presbyterian as early as 1819 expressed his disappointment because the circus had received so much support that it went beyond its scheduled engagement in the village of

Chillicothe.[16] Editors denounced the circus on many grounds. It competed with the churches for funds in support of benevolence. The circus promoted idleness, intemperance, vulgarity, vice, and degradation. The obscenity and ribaldry, the indecent dress of the performers, especially that of the female equestrians, and their "disgusting" postures could lead the young to possible fatal moral injury. "The gilded chariots—the swelling music—the artificial fool—the parade of men and horses, are well calculated to ensnare and lead captive the unsophisticated heart of youth."[17]

Most clergymen found little that was amusing or attractive in the career of P. T. Barnum, the leading showman of his day. He had almost won his way into some hearts for his temperance lectures and because of a report that he refused publicly to accept a drink of wine.[18] It was a Catholic editor who believed the report was a hoax by which Barnum expected to overcome religious prejudice toward him in the community. The same editor ridiculed Barnum's "*half-dead*-heart-broken looking lions and tigers, as also those outrageous, rickety imitations of humanity in wax."[19] Barnum's financial failure in the 1850's came as no surprise to those who believed "in a special Providence." A Universalist, however, professed sympathy for Barnum in view of the fact that his failure had allegedly resulted from being swindled by an orthodox Christian.[20]

The performing arts were rarely, if ever, judged by Protestant churchmen on the basis of their cultural or artistic value, but rather on the basis of their moral effects. The Sunday evening concerts in the German coffee houses of Cincinnati where there was "nigger singing," drinking, and boisterousness, and the operas with their cast of foreigners who were deficient in "moral and religious culture," received the scorn of Methodist editors.[21] Fanny Elssler may have enraptured easterners with her classical ballet, but not editors of religious papers in the Northwest.

A Methodist Protestant was frightened by the extravagance of the public enthusiasm for her, which had even led a group of enthralled young men to unhitch the horses from her carriage so that they could pull it to her hotel. This enthusiasm he regarded as one of the most "detestable instances of human folly and degradation that our nature is capable of."[22]

Perhaps the most curious reaction to any form of amusement was a secular paper's comment on the lowly organ grinder in the streets of Cincinnati. This "street opera" attracted the "vicious boys and profane loafers . . . whose lewd and indecent remarks" were an annoyance to respectable citizens. While a local Presbyterian did not argue with the criticism, he wondered why his lay colleague did not attack the local theater, a much more serious evil.[23]

There was perhaps the nearest to unanimity on a moral issue among all religions, exclusive of the Jews, on the evils of the theater. The *Israelite* advertised the theater and the opera, urged attendance, and editorially defended them. Wise criticized the American churches for their failure to realize that the theater in Europe was, with a few exceptions, a proper school of morals and a means of elevating the tastes of the masses. In America, however, materialism had corrupted the theater, spoiling both the tastes and morals reflected in it. Wise specifically objected to some anti-Semitic titles and to the idealization of the prostitute in some American theater, but reform of the theater, not its interdiction, was the answer.[24]

The editor of the *Catholic Telegraph* did not accept the theater as historically evil but he agreed with Protestants that the "intellectual, as well as the moral standard of the stage, is sunken utterly below the hope of an elevation worthy the genius which has adorned and enabled the histrionic art." The Catholic Church, he wrote, condemned the theater on the grounds of its subject matter, the off-stage conduct of actors and actresses, the exposure of the

71

person, the pandering to the tastes of the rabble, obscenity in the dialogue, and the baseness of those who attended.[25] Such characteristics of the theater conditioned the disapproval of churchmen of all faiths for many years.[26] Protestant objections were essentially the same as those published in the *Telegraph*. One additional objection pertained to the artificial and exaggerated emotions created by the drama which gave "in a night as much of passion, as the current of life would furnish in a year."[27] The theater not only coated vice with fascination but in its wake it attracted saloons and prostitutes.[28] Dramatizations of *Uncle Tom's Cabin,* while destined to help gain approval for the theater, were nevertheless taboo even among many radically antislavery editors.[29]

A very mixed reaction came from religious newspapers upon the occasion of the visit of the great Swedish singer, Jenny Lind, to the United States, 1850-1851, through the agency of P. T. Barnum. Her vast charities in Europe and in the United States, including a $1500 gift to the Lutheran Capital University, along with her very proper conduct, her talent, and her natural attractiveness, made her difficult to dislike even within the framework of the narrow moralism of the age.[30] Many reacted unfavorably, however, to the excitement and acclaim with which the public received her, referring to the phenomenon as the "Jenny Lind mania." Others objected to the exorbitant proceeds from her appearances, perhaps envious of the $14,000 to $50,000 per concert. Always objectionable, of course, was the fact that the scene of most of her concerts was a theater building.[31]

Exhibitions in the area of natural or industrial science often found warm acceptance among editors, as did the county or state agricultural fairs which became common during the era. The fairs were lauded because they united the people of the state, they gave evidence of God's ministrations, they helped elevate and dignify labor, and they helped agriculture become more progressive.[32]

Editors soon came to object, however, to the entertainment features which appeared as these enterprises became more commercial and sophisticated. A Lutheran voiced the objection of many to the female equestrians who "divest themselves of all modesty" and succumb to the love of applause instead of preparing for the quiet pleasures of home. Also deplored was the "Baby Show," a possible forerunner of the beauty pageant, as a new feature of the fairs. It was obnoxious for mothers to put themselves and their babies "up before the rude gaze of the public, an exhibition for the mere temporary gratification of vain pride or for filthy lucre."[33]

Much literature was outside the rigid requirements of seriousness of purpose, moral purity, and truth demanded for any use of time by a Christian. This was almost universally true of novels. Not even *Uncle Tom's Cabin* set aside all misgiving, since some thought it unfortunate that the case against slavery should be put in fictional form. No element of the Christian editorial corps was prepared for the realism and social reflection in some of the novels of European authors at this time. Reactions to Bulwer-Lytton were typical. His work was so vile that no words could describe it in spite of its "elegance of composition." When he came to the United States with his paramour, he called forth the abuse of one editor who found the unprincipled life of the author as "licentious as his books." A Universalist contrasted Bulwer-Lytton with novelists whose stories elevated the mind, purified the affections, and sustained domestic life. He acknowledged the author's genius and his "deep insight into human nature—its motives, passions, and springs of action; yet one can hardly read his works—at least I cannot—without the most painful sensations, although with all-absorbing interest."[34] In another age this might have been part of a formula for establishing the validity of literature.

The reception of Charles Dickens and his novels was also generally frigid. According to a Catholic, "Dickens has so long indulged in fiction that he knows not how to tell truth and he has so long looked on human life for whatever is ridiculous, that he is obliged, by the force of an evil habit, to treat whatever is grave and solemn with the senseless levity of a buffoon."[35] As usual, Dickens' domestic life was included in an evaluation of his work. His separation from his wife in 1858 was the logical result of the life of a novelist with Dickens' less than adequate religious principles. It had followed "a scandalous family brawl between parties who are equally nervous, fidgety, and unprincipled."[36]

One Methodist, and he was very much alone among Methodists, found comfort in the fact that the reading habits of Americans were improving because they were showing interest in such authors as Walter Scott and James Fenimore Cooper. Much more normal was the reaction of a colleague who found it a waste of "shining talents" for a man like Scott to be devoted to the novel. Another Methodist held William Makepeace Thackery in complete contempt. He called his lecture in Cincinnati in 1856 "the greatest humbug we ever witnessed." It was a "string of twaddle — a recital of some very silly stories about a very silly monarch.... The meaningless superficiality of the lecture was one of the direct fruits of man's giving himself wholly up to the work of fiction writing."[37]

Late in the 1840's normally warring factions in Cincinnati were drawn together when editions of Dickens, Alexander Dumas, and Bulwer-Lytton made their appearance in "dirty, dingy pamphlet form."[38] The Catholic editor pledged himself to co-operate with the "sectarians" who were trying to arouse public sentiment against these and other obscene books available along the waterfront. He could not resist pointing out, however, that the public mind had been prepared for such a pernicious feast by mothers who had permitted "their children to read the scandalous and unchaste imaginings of Maria Monk" a decade before.[39] A jingoistic westerner pointed with satisfaction to the report that a local publisher had to go East to get some obscene drawings engraved because "our young Cincinnati artists, poor as they are, could not be seduced with 500 dollars, cash in hand."[40]

The churchmen of the West generally frowned upon any frivolous observance of the national holiday on July 4. Among the "acts of folly" meriting editorial scoldings were "silly toasts and bacchanalian songs," pompous and superpatriotic speeches, cannon firing, excessive drinking, "swearing, fighting, gambling, horse-racing . . . and every description of wickedness."[41] Protestants happily solved these problems by sanctifying the day to a religious purpose. Elaborate Sunday School exercises thoroughly blended devotional purposes and patriotism to show the young the intimate connection between the Protestant religion and good government. Religious activities also kept those in attendance from otherwise "mingling in scenes of revelry and dissipation."[42] On the whole Catholic editors welcomed the celebration as an opportunity to exhibit for all to see their appreciation for the values of republican government.[43]

The observance of Christmas was either severely qualified or totally despised by most Protestants. A Presbyterian typically saw Christmas as of heathen and Catholic origin. The "idleness, festivity, nonsense, and wickedness" associated with the holiday also condemned it. Both religion and patriotism supported the denunciation. "Our country is Protestant. Why should we appear, on the 25th of December, like France, Italy, or Austria which are covered with clouds of superstition and ignorance?"[44]

The one really holy day was the Sabbath, the proper observance of which was a leading religious and moral concern of the editors of religious papers. Some even feared that subscribers might read the nonreligious sections of their papers on the Sabbath. The Sabbatarian emphasis characterized every Protestant group including those from national cultures which had, by custom, a broader view of the Sabbath.[45] In fact, churches with German constituencies seem to emphasize deliberately the issue to show that they were orthodox American in this respect. There was among them a marked sensitivity to the injustice done to German immigrants by natives who drew general conclusions from the behavior of "the peculiarly boisterous Red Republican portion of our German immigrants."[46]

Common elements in the theology of the Sabbath among the orthodox were the threat of punishment for those who did not properly observe the Sabbath and better health and more prosperity for those who did. When lightning struck a barn full of hay near Chillicothe, the editor of the *Weekly Recorder* accused the owner of having stored the hay on the Sabbath and he refused to accept the farmer's denial that this was the case. Later when a young man drowned in the Scioto River on the Sabbath, the incident provided another opportunity to moralize about the punishment awaiting those who ignored the sacredness of the day. Ironically, the editor's own nineteen-year old son was later drowned on a Tuesday evening while swimming in the Scioto.[47] There was no hint as to what corresponding deviation from God's law had brought this catastrophe to John Andrews' own household.

The very rapid growth of travel facilities, of commercial enterprise, and of government mail service in the Northwest presented the major challenges to proper Sabbath observance. Traveling on the Sabbath led to accidents which were of "God's appointment," according to an Episcopalian. A Presbyterian went much further. He warned those railroads which refused to suspend their services completely on the Sabbath that God would "permit them to employ swindlers, and to buy wheels and axles with flaws," nor would He "restrain the wind from falling trees upon their tracks." One young Presbyterian minister returning from his general assembly died of cholera because he went aboard a boat on Sunday, his only excuse being that he had to meet an appointment to be married. *"Is there not a God?"* were the concluding words of the *Oberlin Evangelist's* description of this incident.[48]

Protestant agreement that the state should force the citizens to keep the Sabbath[49] was sharply challenged. The editor of the Universalist *Star* angrily wrote: "This has always been the political faith of the Puritans. Whenever they have formed a majority in any government, they have hunted down the minority as a set of outlawed rebels, or as beasts of prey." The editor of the *Star* also assaulted the "hypocritical vanity" of those who encouraged the Sabbath-keeping "religious stages, steam boats, canal packets, etc.," as the orthodox so often did.[50] While Catholics also dwelt fondly upon Protestant inconsistencies, the editor in Cincinnati did agree that disregard of the Sabbath and intemperance were the leading causes of increased crime. He would "go as far as any Protestant" in Sabbath reform, including support for the "most stringent laws against the desecration of the Sunday, by business and the sale of intoxicating liquors." He commended Catholics who avoided amusements on the Sabbath as a courtesy toward Protestant neighbors.[51] Protestants did often complain bitterly about religious processions and Catholic festivities which disturbed the peace of the Sabbath.

The use of tobacco was common even among the clergy in America in the nineteenth century, a fact which only intensified editors' frequent criticism of its use. A Presbyterian issued the typical objections in 1830. "The habit of chewing, smoking, or snuffing tobacco, is not only disgusting, but it is absolutely sinful. Sinful, because it injures the health of the consumers, and is an altogether useless expenditure of time and money." For a clergyman, whose example was so vital, it was especially sinful.[52] The chewing and spitting of the clergy fouled the place of worship and were an "unspeakable annoyance to all women and all decent men."[53] The "filthy habits" of the Presbyterian clergy even made it difficult to get a meeting place for the General Assembly in 1837.[54] Former users of tobacco acquired a special authority in urging others to desist. A Universalist described himself as having been a complete slave to tobacco for fourteen years before mastering the habit. Editor William Hanby of the United Brethren Church had tried for years to taper off his use of tobacco, but he lost "all taste for the nasty weed" only after a crisis in his religious experience. "The use of tobacco is a filthy curse upon the health of hundreds and thousands of persons and pockets," he wrote. He particularly chided ministers who had to interrupt their sermons in order to spit.[55]

The earliest religious newspapers in the Northwest were concerned with the use of ardent spirits. The editor of the Quaker paper committed himself to the eradication of their use in 1818. The position of Andrews of the *Weekly Recorder* was less definite, emphasizing only "habitual use" of liquor.[56] As early as 1829 newspaper editors in the Northwest challenged the position of the moderate drinker and hailed the prospect of reformation by moral means in connection with the consumption of liquor.[57] Every major Protestant group in the Northwest emphasized personal abstinence from both the sale and use of alcoholic beverages by the middle 1830's. One Presbyterian felt that public opinion in his denomination would even support the exclusion of traffickers and users of ardent spirits from the church. The editors of the Episcopal paper in Ohio were advocates of temperance throughout all phases of the reform, taking sharp issue with Bishop John Henry Hopkins of Vermont who opposed church support for temperance societies. The *Gambier Observer* used every propaganda device available to further the cause and claimed the backing, with

few exceptions, of the Episcopal clergy in the West.[58]
Even as early as 1835 some editors were urging restrictive action by states and municipalities.[59] The climax of the movement for legal prohibition came, however, in the 1850's in the push for some version of the Maine prohibition law in the states of the Northwest. The campaign for such a law in Ohio drew the support of Methodist, Episcopalian, Presbyterian, and German Reformed, among others. The Scandinavian press in Wisconsin and Illinois gave its backing to similar legislation there. The *Kirke Tidende* expected a special gain for Norwegians from such a law. "Our honorable Norwegian national character would no longer be sullied by the loathsome vice of intoxication; for what has degraded our honorable Northmen's reputation more and what has made us more despised among our American fellowmen?"[60] Universalists were less enthusiastic for the cause of temperance, but the editor of the *Star* was converted to prohibition when one of three drunken men whom he met on the road leveled a gun at his head. He thereafter urged his fellow Universalists to openly identify themselves with the temperance cause.[61]

The Roman Catholic Church in the Northwest furnished its share of advocates for both temperance and total abstinence. The *Western Catholic Register,* published in Detroit in the 1840's, was as much temperance as it was Catholic. The *Telegraph* began to carry some temperance items in the 1830's. In 1840, the paper announced the formation of the Roman Catholic Total Abstinence Association of Cincinnati with Bishop Purcell's name at the head of the list of the signers of the pledge. In 1846, the *Telegraph* seemed to endorse rather tentatively some form of legal restraint on the sale of liquor in Cincinnati. Eventually, however, the paper vigorously opposed the Maine law principle as "an out and out unmitigated humbug—a scheme as ridiculous as ever emanated from the fanatical brain" of self righteous Puritans.[62] Protestants generally appreciated the interest of Catholics in temperance reform in view of German and Irish drinking habits. The hostility between Catholics and Protestants eliminated any united effort in behalf of the reform. Many Protestants were openly cynical with respect to Father Theobald Matthew, the famous Irish temperance advocate, and the *Telegraph* warned Catholics to confine their temperance activities entirely to associations within the Catholic Church.[63]

The inherent appeal of sex guaranteed the subject a place in the religious newspaper in spite of the delicacy with which it was usually treated.[64] A particular dilemma arose from a showing in Cincinnati in 1848 of Hiram Powers' celebrated "Greek Slave," a striking statue of a nude female. Barnum's skill in presenting Powers' sculpture may have tempered the bias of the western clergy toward nudity in art, but it did not eliminate it. One editor only, a New School Presbyterian, admitted to having viewed the exhibit in response to a special invitation to the clergy. He was impressed "with the exquisite skill of the sculptor, who could inspire the cold marble with such an appearance of life, sentiment and intellect." The editor acknowledged that his "Puritan conscience must be permitted to question the moral influence of such an exhibition, even at the risk of being thought destitute of taste and cultivation." The Old School editor in the city pointedly refused the invitation to view the exhibit. "No man believes, or can believe, that females could thus exhibit themselves without outraging the feelings of the virtuous and promoting vice in its worst forms." The editor of a local, general newspaper challenged the fitness of ministers who, like this Presbyterian, could not view the "Greek Slave" without having their baser sentiments aroused.[65] The Methodist editor conceded that Powers' choice of subject was excellent. "He has appealed to humanity in two of its strongest principles: the love of sex, and the feeling of pity or compassion" arising from her bondage and her nudity. The feelings awakened by the statue were not necessarily base, but the sculpture, like fiction, inspired only feelings and not useful actions toward the plight of the slave.[66] The only comment of the Catholic editor was to remind Protestants of the inconsistency in being scandalized by the nudity of the sculpture while able to absorb the obscenities of the anti-Catholic lecturers.[67]

Oberlin College and its newspaper, the *Evangelist*, attracted public attention through episodes which involved some of their group in deviant behavior. Oberlin was somewhat on the defensive as far as sex was concerned because of her perfectionism and because the College had pioneered in coeducation. Oberlin's experiment in coeducation was carried out under meticulous scrutiny and her attitudes toward sex were conventional. The staff of the College insisted, however, that bringing the sexes together in education "as rational beings, as fellow students, as *Christian students*" could hardly be an agency in the pollution of morals. Spokesmen for Oberlin also challenged the double standard which made the female suffer socially so much more than the male for sexual promiscuity.[68] One occasion for embarrassment was with a young man in the preparatory division who sent obscene letters and drawings to two of the girls. He was administered twenty-five lashes and told to leave the campus by a group of faculty and students who acted without formal authority, an event critics described as the "Oberlin lynching." The participants elaborately confessed their wrongdoing in this use of violence in an extra of the *Oberlin Evangelist*. "We had ourselves done wrong, and to state what that wrong was, and confess it became a *duty* and a *privilege*." They did offer a defense of their actions on the basis that civil law did not provide for such a case, the offense was so horrifying that their feelings got out of hand, and some of the boys involved in the lynching were brothers of the girls who received the letters.[69]

The principal faculty member involved in the lynching

was H. C. Taylor, who was also editor of the *Evangelist* and acting postmaster. About three years later, by material evidence and by his own confession, Taylor was found guilty of embezzlement from the *Evangelist*, of having taken money from the post office, of having seduced the young woman who came to keep house for him after his wife's death, and of having procured an abortion for her. President Asa Mahan explained the overwhelming sorrow and embarrassment over Taylor's actions. "When the first shock of surprise and horror was over, then the steel entered our souls. We knew what grief was—grief for the cause of holiness, of moral reform, of the Sabbath, of the suffering slave, of every good cause of which he had been the advocate before the world, and this dreadful fall would so deeply wound."[70] Taylor was one of those who had campaigned actively for "moral reform," meaning legislation punishing adultery as a crime. He had been connected with Western Reserve University, where he was chairman of the Committee on Lewdness. In this capacity he had contributed lengthy columns of material which fell just short of naming names in describing details of seductions, adultery, and illegitimate births in the various communities of the Reserve.[71] Both painstaking research and a fevered interest in sexual activity went into these articles which were, in all probability, symptomatic of his own problem.

One of the most notorious of the sex scandals which resulted in violence in that generation was the seduction of the wife of Congressman Daniel Sickles by District Attorney Phillip Barton Key of Washington, D. C., and the subsequent slaying of Key by Sickles. The Methodist editor in Chicago wrote of Sickles that "the manner in which he armed himself and shot his victim in the light of heaven on God's blessed Sabbath-day, is akin to *murder*."[72] Editors found that dancing, which figured so prominently in Washington society, conditioned weak women for just this kind of sin. Some also related the crime more remotely to the moral effects of slavery in the nation's capital.[73] In general, western editors finally did not agree with the jury in ruling the slaying justifiable homicide even though they deemed all parties equally sinful and equally guilty in the crime.

When editors offered advice on the subject of marriage they dealt with such topics as the nature and importance of marriage, imprudent marriage as a source of vice and misery, the fallacy of marrying for beauty or for mercenary considerations, the proper age for marriage, religion in the marriage relations, remarriage after the death of a spouse, and the duties of parents. Instructions in such cases were quite vague.[74] The subject of divorce received relatively more attention. In reality, divorce was not very common anywhere in the United States at that time. In 1860 there were 1.2 divorces for every 1,000 existing marriages, though it seems that divorce was more common in some states of the Northwest. Indiana in particular had acquired a reputation for laxness.[75] All elements of the religious press agreed on the evils of relaxing divorce laws and generally supported the tightening of discipline on divorce within their communions.[76]

Religious newspapers advised in the area of the rearing, moral instruction, and discipline of children. Their own formal columns for children and youth were moralistic, bland, and seldom realistic. Editorial advice, on the other hand, at least showed awareness of the pressures upon family life which appeared in the emerging cities of the Northwest. A Methodist wrote angrily of the "revolutionary spirit abroad in families at the present time, a disposition in children to govern parents, and a palpable defiance of parental authority." This editorial titled, "The New Reign of Order" referring to the "spirit of pompous self-reliance and reckless independence" among the youth, seemed to have the authentic emotions of parenthood behind it and could have been written fresh from a confrontation with a son or daughter of his own.

Others saw a lack of parental training due to the influence of the city leading to "juvenile depravity," so that many boys and girls grew up to be social pests. The Catholic editor in Cincinnati saw in the conservative principles of the Catholic tradition the only force which could save America from the immorality of her own children.[77] Some editors advocated the wisdom of reason, affection, and encouragement as features of discipline.[78] The German Methodist, William Nast, advised his parental readers that the learning process should be accepted as gradual and it should be made attractive. Parents should respect their children and avoid harsh criticism and overly severe discipline, especially with adolescents. His colleague, Elliott, observing a mother's physical and verbal abuse of her child, reflected upon the feelings of hate, and the lives of "meanness and dishonor" which this parental reaction tended to breed.[79]

The male editors of religious newspapers reacted with less than enthusiasm to the claims advanced by and for women in the first half of the nineteenth century. The scriptures and common sense decreed the domestic role of women and their subordination to men in marriage. Women had to be protected from the vulgar, male environment of the polls at election time.[80] Many, however, agreed upon an improved status for working women and the protection of married women in their property rights. They justified the claims of women to equal wages and called for an expansion of employment opportunities for women, especially widows.[81] There was frequent editorial endorsement of major reforms along these lines, including the full right of the wife to her husband's property upon his death, a voice with the husband in all important property transactions, and the right of a woman to hold her own property after marriage.[82]

With the exception of Oberlin personnel, the men were absolutely opposed to women in the pulpit.[83] Oberlin, of course, graduated a pioneer in this field, Miss Antoinette

Brown, though not without some reservations. To Catholics this development, along with the whole women's rights agitation, indicated "the tendency of Protestantism to undo and destroy" all the civilization which the Catholic faith had so laboriously constructed.[84] Editors often greeted the appearance of female reformers on the lecture platform with laughter, albeit suspiciously nervous laughter. A Methodist was impressed with Lucy Stone and her appealing manner, "but, in the language of surly Dr. Johnson, we would say, 'Sir, a woman's speaking is like a dog's walking on its hind legs—it is not done well; but you are surprised to find it done at all'." A Baptist in Michigan cited a very common, if naive, belief of the male clergy regarding a cure for feminine activism. "It is worthy of notice that actual *matrimony has proved an almost infallible cure* for the very worst cases of *women's rights insanity.* Courtship mitigates the symptoms; a direct offer restores a healthy circulation of feminine ideas; the wedding usually completes the cure." If any "morbid notions" remained, then certainly the maternal instinct would eliminate them.[85]

Men discussed women's fashions both seriously and with tongue in cheek. There was no use, according to a Presbyterian, for "superfluous ribbons, costly laces, ridiculous bonnets, and the bravery of useless jewels." The use of hoops convinced men of the vanity and weakmindedness of women as they watched the awkward maneuvering of hoop skirts into church pews or into train seats. Most editors sensed, however, that any crusade against them was useless. "O knight of rashness!" wrote a Methodist in reply to a reader who had asked his editor to launch a war against them. This Methodist vindicated hoops, though, on the basis that they sustained for a woman "a similar relation to that of the *cowcatcher* to the *locomotive.* They certainly have a tendency to clear the track."[86]

The religious newspapers of the Northwest were substantially identified with efforts to reduce violence and brutality. Dueling was absolutely condemned by every editor. Accounts of crimes of violence, suicides, and executions were, on the other hand, standard fare in the nonreligious segments of their papers. All of the more sensational murder cases were the subject of much moralizing relative to temperance, erroneous theology, extravagant living, or occasionally, the unnecessary prevalence and use of firearms. The editors' own sense of morbidity or of duty usually overcame any misgivings about descriptions of criminal acts in their papers. One editor frankly stated that he wanted to know for himself the details of these affairs, that he assumed others did, and that no harm would result from this knowledge. Not only that, but for those who, in the future, studied the events of the time, "some idea might be formed of the spirit of our day."[87] For this the historian will bow appreciatively in his direction.

The practice of executing criminals in public received widespread and decidedly negative comment in religious papers. The editor of the *Western Christian Advocate* was one of the clergy who attended the public hanging of a murderer in Cincinnati in 1837 in order, as always, to "improve it, if possible, for moral purposes." He described the last conversation in the cell, the bearing of the prisoner, the emotional farewells, the huge crowd estimated at 15,000, the hymn, the prayer, and the prisoner's address. The prisoner, in what must have been his finest hour, described for the public his descent into hell by way of "disregard of parental authority, Sabbath breaking, intemperance, theft, robbery and murder." In spite of the utility of the scene for him, the editor concluded "that public executions are a great evil" for instead of striking fear into the heart of the potential criminal, the public spectacle tended to immunize against that fear.[88]

Some reformers went on to challenge capital punishment. Michigan in 1847 became the first state in the United States to abolish the death penalty and Wisconsin became the third to do so in 1853. This was done without the support of the editors of religious newspapers. The only ones to question the death penalty were the Quakers and the Universalists, with the Quakers having no newspaper at the time the reform occurred. A Universalist editor summarized the attitude of his group toward capital punishment. "We deem it a practice unworthy a Christian people, being productive of no good, but an abundance of evil. It cannot repair the injury done, nor reform the offender, neither is it a salutary means of deterring others from the commission of the same offense."[89] For the overwhelming majority of Protestants, God's law required this form of retribution.[90] Misplaced concern for the criminal was contrary to the health of the body politic because it showed "sympathy with sin, rather than its innocent and righteous victim."[91] Editors were certain that murders were more numerous because of the move to abolish the death penalty and because juries tended to render acquittal when the death penalty was involved.[92] The fact that innocent men were sometimes hanged was no argument against legal executions. "It is simply an argument against hanging innocent men."[93] The *Catholic Telegraph* joined Protestants in accepting hanging as a deterrent to crime. The editor charged that the "No Hell—No Hanging" morality in America accounted for a long catalogue of criminal behavior including the Mormon iniquity, New England free love, ridicule of Christianity, infanticide, abortion, and mass murder.[94]

Prizefighting in its most brutal form made its clandestine appearance in the United States during the late 1840's. Even though these bouts were generally staged abroad or in the East, they drew the wrath of western editors. The bare-knuckled fights understandably received such labels as brutal, savage, semi-barbaric, and degraded, and the participants were called the "bullies of the ring." In this instance the *Israelite* might well have been a spokesman for Christian morality. Wise shamed England where some of these fights were staged, shamed the American people, and shamed the telegraphers who relayed the news. "Gentlemen of respectability, together with loafers and bullies run to the newspaper offices to hear about the fight; talk first and last of the great fight .... Never has moral poverty demonstrated itself in a clearer light."[95]

More than a century ago, at least a few Americans challenged the commercialization of burial practices then emerging in urban areas of the United States. Some religious papers had contributed to this trend themselves by advertising expanded services including "patent, metallic, burial cases" endorsed by Whigs and Democrats alike, i.e., by Henry Clay, Daniel Webster, and Lewis Cass.[96] The Catholic press admitted and condemned the public scandal sometimes associated with Catholic funerals. A long line of carriages filled with drunken, laughing, shouting mourners was hardly a Christian display, and the editor of the *Telegraph* warned that if his public notice of the problem became necessary again he would name names "in order that they may take the responsibility of their bad conduct, and not allow it to rest on the great body of the Catholic population." All the widows and orphans of the city, he insisted, could be supported from the costs of the vulgar displays of vanity at funerals.[97] A Lutheran opposed the new practices not only for economic reasons but attributed the bereaved's reaction to social pressure rather than to any genuinely soothing potential in the costly casket linings, shrouds, white gloves, and carriages furnished by the entrepreneur. The rich, he advised, because they could afford any cost, might set an impressive Christian example by refusing to contract for fancy funerals.[98] Many urged that burials not be made during the Sabbath in order to avoid distracting persons from public worship and to avoid requiring anyone to dispense a professional service on that day.[99]

Although some of these issues implied some form of political action, most editors saw them within the framework of the method of "moral suasion." There was another category of public questions, however, which involved choices of specific political action and upon which editors expressed their opinions. Ultimately most editors openly crossed the boundary which restrained them from a political role. They, on occasion and sometimes frequently, surveyed political and economic issues and institutions, politicians and their behavior, the political process itself, public education, foreign policy, and even community problems.

Chapter V
PUBLIC POLICIES IN THE AGE
OF THE COMMON MAN

The years 1814-1861 saw the Northwest vitally involved in all of the profound changes then transforming the United States. Territorial expansion, sectional conflict, industrialization, immigration, and urbanization created the requirement for more adequate public policies in dealing with internal improvements, land sales, banking and currency regulation, tariffs, and the social problems of civil disorder, poverty, and depressions. Political institutions and educational policies were shifting rapidly in the direction of the common man. The clergy, as did the rest of the population, suffered from a lack of experience with these realities and a lack of systematic study of the functions of political, social, and economic institutions. This lack did not deter editors from attempting to measure public policies by the moral law of God while disclaiming any political or partisan interest.

These men seldom considered democracy and political reform in the abstract and never systematically. They generally supported or took for granted the propriety of universal manhood suffrage, but they were otherwise cool toward many of the political emphases in Jacksonian democracy. There was little understanding of and much less appreciation for the party discipline which developed under Jackson, since it was deemed to be at variance with Christianity, injurious to the nation, and self-defeating.[1] The spoils system, rather than being welcomed as an agency of party discipline and political reform, was considered to be the ultimate degradation wherein "ability, integrity, virtue, and honesty" were destroyed.[2] In retrospect, one man viewed the extraordinary power which Jackson had acquired through his popularity with the people, not as an instrument of democracy, but as "highly dangerous to the republic."[3] There

was little understanding of the change in nominating procedures from the caucus to the national convention and
its practical relationship to democracy.

Any open comment on Andrew Jackson himself tended
to reflect the New England clerics' old Federalist bias.
Even before Jackson attained the presidency, a Presbyterian was rebuking Jackson's temper, his dueling, and
the "joyful" celebration on the Sabbath of his return
from the Indian wars. Providing an ironic twist to democracy, he saw the hero as a "worm of the dust" who
dared not dishonor God in profaning the Sabbath any
more than anyone else.[4] The Plan of Union paper on the
Western Reserve was the only paper, however, to get
involved in election politics in 1828. It did so because
of the editor's conviction that the election of Jackson
would destroy the nation. During the campaign he carried
an elaborate summary of a defamatory pamphlet based
upon the irregularities in Rachael Jackson's divorce from
her previous husband. His only criticism of the material
was the author's "air of triumph" over and lack of compassion for the adulterous Jackson.[5]

Religious papers consistently criticized the party politics of the Jackson era as incompatible with the Christian
profession. There was a dilemma, however, for those
who felt that they had a responsibility to influence the
political process but found that process itself abhorrent.
The editor of the Methodist paper in Cincinnati could not
bring himself to say that a Christian lost his innocence in
acting through political parties but he believed that piety
declined when church members were involved in political
divisions and campaign activities. Nevertheless, when Elliott became disillusioned with the policies of the Tyler
administration, he lashed the pious who had refused to
participate in grass roots politics. "By their *negligence,*
there is repudiation, bank frauds, dishonest insolvencies,
a bad currency, improper credit, etc., etc." Instead of
Christians combining to capture primary meetings "they

had come to the *unchristian* conclusion that Christians have little, or nothing, to do with elections and sober political meetings."[6]

There was unusual nervousness among editors during the election campaigns because the excitement distracted church members from religious pursuits.[7] The exaggerated aspersions on the character of opponents destroyed kind feelings, and cultivated "all the evil passions of the human heart."[8] A Universalist, fearing the campaign's disruptive effects, penned in exasperation in 1840: "If you want to build 'log cabins,' do it; if you want to 'hurrah for Van Buren!' do it; but do not let it break up your Christian fellowship and intercourse."[9] Campaigns were thought to be wasteful of money, to be destructive of morals among the young onlookers, and to reduce the respect of the people for their leaders.[10]

The moral qualifications of both the candidate and party were always the foremost consideration at election time. Only by the absolute refusal of Christians to accept one of two unsatisfactory candidates would the parties learn to nominate moral men for office.[11] A Methodist called for all persons of real moral worth to come out of both parties and consolidate among themselves in order to control policy for moral ends. The failure to do so had, among other evil results, allowed immigrants to combine under a foreign influence and hold a balance of power so that nearly illiterate "canal-diggers" could control the descendents of pilgrims.[12] The latter was ironic since editor Elliott had himself come from Ireland as a lad.

The editors of religious papers faced far more deviant political behavior than that adopted by the Whigs and Democrats in their efforts to propagandize the masses. They were uniformly intolerant of Thomas Dorr and his followers who sought to reform the suffrage by force in Rhode Island in the 1840's. A Methodist Protestant labeled Dorr a scoundrel worthy of the penitentiary if not the halter. A Presbyterian rejected as spurious Dorr's appeal to the American Revolution as a precedent for the use of violence to achieve justice. In the new era, any changes in government could only proceed from existing authority and without violence, recklessness, or mob action.[13] "All mobs in a country where the majority rule, are wrong; essentially and immutably wrong; in every sense of the word they are wicked and bad," stormed a Methodist.[14] Civil disorder in the form of mob violence was, in fact, a very common feature of the age. There were race riots, election day riots, anti-Catholic riots, anti-abolition riots, and antibank riots, to name a few. The prevalence of mob action was one of the few characteristics of the epoch which took the edge from clerical editors' optimism. The growing spirit of anarchy and individual resistance to law indicated man's tendency to throw off all restraints until violence was checked only by its own extravagance.[15]

There was no uniform response to the socialist variations from American norms in theory and in practice. George W. Harris, a Michigan Baptist, was one who felt that the socialistic schemes at least attempted to cope with real and serious problems. "There is cause sufficient in the condition of the poor, in the issue between labor and capital, in the burdens likely to be imposed upon us by a large class of foreigners, destitute of means, and wanting a general industrial education, to give great practical interest and importance" to the discussion of socialism. Supply and demand were, however, valid economic forces and to make war on capital was to make war on labor as well. The role of the Christian moralist was, therefore, both to recognize the worth of capital and to "more effectively distribute its blessings."[16]

Occasionally an editor looked with an open mind, if not with favor, upon the schemes of the utopian socialists to reform society by communitarian examples. Epaphras Goodman, a reform-minded Presbyterian, gave a positive account of the Fourierist, Roxburg Community. In general, he thought that labor might be more productive and expenses less severe under the phalanx system. This type of community might also be able to effectively regulate morality but only extensive experimentation could confirm or deny its possibilities for good. At least two Universalist editors had been members of Fourierist communities. The editor in Alphadelphia, Michigan, was relieved, however, to be free from the "effort to unite such discordant materials" as those on the one hand who were interested in money only and those on the other hand who were interested primarily in principle. His colleague in Ohio felt that the movement had not retained its religious spirit and, since the Gospel of Jesus Christ alone was "the power of God unto salvation from social ills," socialists of this type were trying to build a house without a foundation.[17]

It was the rule, however, for the churchmen to reject even the nonviolent planners. They condemned Robert Owen, Frances Wright, and others largely because of their departures from Christian orthodoxy. Churchmen could not overlook the communitarians' disregard for the concept of original sin which, in both the softened forms of Calvinism and in the Arminian theology of Methodism, stressed the depravity of natural man. If the idea of the community of goods was not actually a humbug or a fraud for the benefit of the organizers,[18] then it could be counted on to fail anyway because it was futile to attempt to reform society without first redeeming men from their natural, sinful state.[19]

The Catholic press was particularly hostile to all forms of socialism. The Church taught obedience, love of peace, and disinterestedness according to its voice in Cincinnati. Socialism in contrast, breathed hatred, accused God of evil, and made of every individual a tyrant who thought he had a right to prey on the community. The only real equality was that of every man's accountability to God and in the requirement of the ruler to rule

well and the subject to obey well. Socialists excited re-
bellions, created anarchy, glutted themselves with plun-
der, and reveled in the blood of rulers. Only the triumph
of Catholic institutions across the world could secure
men from this universal confusion.[20]

In spite of the general antipathy toward schemes for
reordering society, some men with the less affluent constituents showed an acute class sensitivity and expressed
some deep personal resentment. The Millerite publication
threatened both rich churches and rich men with the
millenial climax to history. Its editor was fiercely critical
of the "Last Day Treasures" of the Methodist Book
Concern, meaning its accumulated property of $650,000,
while the poor of the Methodist Church were persecuted
"for not paying up their class money."[21] John Lawrence,
editor of the *Religious Telescope,* which served a generally poor, rural constituency at the time, attacked the
"morbid covetousness" of landlords who charged excessive rents or refused entirely to rent to widows because "It Don't Pay." He pleaded for consideration for
poor prisoners who, in spite of their crimes, were no
worse than the "thousands of other persons" who were
free but who had been more skillful in cheating and who
were still rich and respected after their crimes. The working people were the "bone and sinew" of civilization and
the hope of the church since the masses only "can be
made truly Christian." The workingmen would find a
different route to heaven from that which the elegantly
furnished churches with their godless choirs and godless,
fashionable ministers could provide. Lawrence described
vividly his literal hatred for the idle and fashion-conscious
offspring of the rich, and he was by no means convinced
that they had souls as worthy objects for Christian love.[22]

Many editors went to some lengths to express their
appreciation for the diversity of class interests while re-
taining complete confidence in the existing economic and
social system. A German Reformed editor defended the

working people in their right to explain their distinctive interests through a periodical, the *Western Mechanic*. He also defended their right to demonstrate in protest against unfair practices. He believed it a great credit to the workingman, however, that he remained patriotic and moderate and accepted the right of property even though capital was often used to supplant him with the machine.[23] The Methodist, Elliott, along with other publishers in Cincinnati, had his own labor problems in 1853. Members of the Typographical Union quit work when three Cincinnati publishers refused to agree to a new wage scale. The Union members paraded by and cheered those establishments, apparently including Elliott's, which had agreed to terms. Elliott was entirely good natured and tolerant of the demonstration. He believed that labor had its rights along with capital and declared that he would be inclined to give labor the benefit of the doubt. Though strikes were generally unproductive of public good, he granted that "error," meaning social conflict, was "inseparable from the best steps in human improvement."[24]

Catholics reflected the practical interests of their constituents among the working classes. The *Western Tablet* complained bitterly of unkept promises, filthy living conditions, and brutal foremen in connection with the Chicago Railroad Company which was laying track at Deer Grove, Illinois. The editor of the *Catholic Telegraph* challenged the Protestant press to help the working people who "are manifesting by their 'strikes' the sufferings they are enduring," by honestly reporting the grievances of working people. The *Telegraph* also challenged revivalists to preach to the directors and stockholders of the Marietta Railroad in Ohio and persuade them to pay the wages owed their employees.[25]

Below the struggling working classes were those so impoverished as to be objects of charity. According to ministerial editors, society naturally divided itself into rich and poor because of differences in genius and circumstances, and it was thought to be a "flagrant act of injustice" to equalize property arbitrarily.[26] Editors usually accounted for poverty on the basis of ignorance and vice and, in keeping with their mission, waged war upon these roots.[27] But an editor of the *Religious Telescope,* probably because of his practical experience as overseer of the poor in Circleville, Ohio, significantly qualified this view. The poor were not universally wicked, lazy, or prone to theft. It was difficult, one wrote, "for the human heart to love and have virtue while in tatters and rags."[28] Whatever the causes of poverty or the merits of the poor, editors generally believed that charity toward them was essential. A Methodist Protestant felt that the *innocent* poor had a greater natural right to the necessities than the rich did to their excess wealth, although he was by no means implying that the state should be an agency for the redistribution of wealth. Justice and charity required the rich to supply voluntarily as much employment and the best wages possible and then to assume the burden of poor relief where necessary.[29]

In spite of some obvious problem areas, most of the editors in the Northwest emphatically endorsed the institutional forms gathering shape in the American economy of their generation, and sought only to improve their moral quality. The typical editor felt that he had the best of both the material and spiritual worlds to offer to his readers. He was critical, however, of extravagance in personal living, of consciously adopting wealth as a goal, of using evil means of acquiring wealth such as handling liquor, and of the hoarding of money rather than investing the surplus in good works.[30] The *Israelite* actually saw positive moral values, which the Christian churches themselves had failed to produce, emerging from commercial activity. "Money had done more for the removal of all kinds of prejudices and drawbacks, than many other institutions, created for the same purpose." Men's common desire for money and the need for co-operative effort in producing it forced the yielding of prejudice simply because it was impractical to allow it to affect business relationships. Eventually the entire human race would be "cosmopolitized" and purified through the conduct of business. The Jews would play a proud role in a process whereby material interests would become the "pacificator" of the world and bring a new era in civilization.[31]

There were many Protestant editors who found it especially easy to convert business to religious ends in the late 1840's and 1850's, perhaps because the business community became associated with the revivals of the period. This interest produced such editorial titles as "Glorifying God in Business," "Bible Morality Applied to Business Transactions," "Prosperity in Business," "The Religion of the Sewing Machine," "Business a Discipline," and "Christ and Commerce."[32] These editorials contained nothing profoundly disturbing to the position of the entrepreneur. Business, although a special test of a man's character as well as of his skill, was a test which he could pass readily by means of scrupulous honesty, the faithful honoring of all contracts, the careful control of his feelings toward competitors, and a commitment to abstract justice and the general good. In the most elaborate of these discussions, a Presbyterian underscored the rewards for passing the test: *"If all men would pursue their avocations upon Scriptural principles, they would very generally prosper, and would rarely if ever become bankrupt."*[33] The church as an institution would prosper also. The agrarian might supply strength of character for the country but the new entrepreneur would provide the money for the building of the institutions and property of religion in America.[34]

In business themselves, the proprietors of religious newspapers had a vested interest generally in a stable prosperity and in sound banking and currency policies. The basic frame of reference on these issues continued to be editors' concepts of personal and social morality.

Most agreed, therefore, that repudiation of public debts was simply immoral. Although many editors conceded the necessity of paper money to augment the shortage of specie, there was a general caution and a vaguely expressed desire for effective regulation of the quality of money with no significant suggestion as to how it might be done.[35] Most editors agreed that the action of the mobs who attacked the property of "some four shin plaster banks" in Cincinnati in 1842 was not the proper method of regulating currency, although there were hints of sympathy with the crowds. The editor of the *Western Christian Advocate* used the occasion to point out the need for banking institutions, but he held the individual bankers responsible for honest banking practices. Not quite satisfied with this, he recommended legislative action at some level of the people's choice "to prevent intriguing and irresponsible men from such important undertakings." The Catholic editor could not justify the conduct of either the mobs or the bankers, but he voiced his "secret satisfaction" that this direct action might have solved the problem of worthless currency in Cincinnati.[36]

Those in charge of religious newspapers were generally hurt badly in loss of subscriptions and collections by panics such as those of 1837 and 1857. The causes of panics were listed variously as speculation, an unfavorable balance of trade, imported luxuries, overextension of credit, overproduction, fast living, low morals in the world of trade, vice, demagoguery, misgovernment, and corruption. The most common prescription was retrenchment, especially in the purchase of imported luxuries. Retrenchment might call for the discharge of household employees but never for depriving families of the moral and intellectual diet of the religious newspaper.[37] One cure for overproduction, especially of textiles, was to send missionaries to instruct natives in the use of shirts and breeches.[38]

On the several policies of special economic value to the

Northwest, the editors of religious newspapers found conscience in accord with regional interests. Editors, including Catholics,[39] endorsed specific legislation in favor of a liberal land distribution policy whether in the form of preemption laws, veterans' land acts, or homestead bills. Those who expressed themselves on the tariff question usually did so incidentally but favorably to the protection principle. There was uniform support for internal improvements which included warm approval for public financing through land grants of both local and transcontinental railroads. It was common for editors to urge a vote for local bond issues and to protest vehemently the defeat in Congress or the veto of legislation in behalf of transcontinental projects.[40] Railroad management carefully wooed editors of religious papers by giving them special rates and inviting them on free excursions, with the editors obliging with glowing accounts of the railroads and their great economic, social, and moral value to the nation.

This early romance ended when railroads became less generous with reduced rates for the clergy and for travel to religious conventions. Loud editorial complaints followed both the cancellation of these privileges and what were considered unfair or unwise raises in fares.[42] Perhaps this development helped at least two editors to sense a menacing feature in the concentration of power in railroad corporations. The monopoly potential of the railroad was so great for a German Reformed editor as to be "a new element in . . . political and social organization" for weal or woe. He suggested no more than voluntary self-discipline, however. A Presbyterian also warned that railroads had "so grown in the control of capital and labor, of commerce and travel, that it will prove a great blessing, or a grievous curse, according to its management."[43]

Editors were especially critical of railroads and steamship companies for the high incidence of fatal accidents.

They placed the blame on both operating personnel and management, although some thought that the American public seemed too willing to sacrifice life and limb to get somewhere more quickly or to get goods more cheaply.[44] One paper warned the "slaughter-house companies" of an imminent, divine retribution as well as eternal punishment in spite of the fact that corporations did not have "one neck, so that we could legally chop it off or halter it." A Lutheran suggested a temporal remedy. "If the interests of railroad companies will not prove a sufficient inducement to produce the requisite caution, the strong arm of the law should compel them to provide the means of security."[45] Generally, however, the religious press looked to the power of God, not the power of government to regulate and discipline economic interests.

Educational reform was advancing in the Northwest although somewhat unevenly, just as religious newspapers became an important presence in the region. Nearly all Protestant editors were such ardent advocates of the system of common schools that, if their advocacy carried any weight at all, they helped give birth to public education in the Northwest. Editors, whatever their own educational background, usually regarded the cultivation of practical intelligence, if not intellect, on a par with, or second only to, "the fear of the Lord." Their theoretical justification for this emphasis was the blend of common sense, nationalism, and morality common to most Americans. The public schools were the most effective agency in developing the virtue and intelligence required to support the civil institutions of a free society.[46] Equality of opportunity for children of the rich and the poor in America would result from universal, free, and improved education.[47]

Editors used their papers as vehicles in alerting readers to key issues in elections, urging them to vote to assure the utmost improvement of the schools in physical facilities, teachers, teaching methods, and teacher training. Among the most earnest supporters of the public schools were the editors of the *Western Christian Advocate*. In 1838 its editor told Methodist preachers to become familiar with state laws, participate in the election of officers, serve as one if elected, keep informed of all developments in education, preach sermons on education, and inspire the organization of school districts. Methodists would be directly accountable to God, warned the editor, if 1,866 travelling preachers, 4,717 local preachers, and 423,450 members did not "make the common schools of the West all that they ought to be."[48]

Not only did these gentlemen support the public schools in general but they offered much specific advice on their operation. Teachers must have a "broad, solid, thorough education directed by good sense, aided by some good advice and some observation, and by tact and skill derived from personal experience."[49] Churchmen assumed that teachers must have both moral principle and religious faith. It was entirely necessary for the Cincinnati school board to reject the application of a disciple of Tom Paine since the applicant would be committed to the destruction of "all the institutions of morality and religion."[50] Just as clearly, a young lady "who thinks more of her curls and her jewelry, or her dress and her beaux, than of her responsibilities as a teacher . . . ; who will read novels, write love letters, and dress her hair, and eat sweet meats in the school room," could hardly teach well.[51]

There was some tendency among editors of all faiths in the urban environment of Cincinnati to take a moderate view of educational method and discipline. Rabbi Wise expounded upon what were later to be described as progressive methods in education. "According to our idea all primary readers and spelling books should consist of small and interesting sentences, systematically arranged, and the pupils should, in the first place, learn sentences, and not dead letters." Wise did, however, despise the utilitarian emphasis in American life and learning and this was his chief criticism of the public schools at all levels.[52] The Methodist editor believed that some old methods of discipline were overly harsh if not barbarous. He invited those who opposed all corporal punishment, however, to manage a room of fifty mischievous children and thereby determine for themselves whether or not children were always governable by reason, love, and virtue. On the other hand, the *Advocate* opposed any extension of the school day or of the school week, insisting that it was not healthy for either teachers or pupils to be seated too long upon uncomfortable chairs in crowded, ill-ventilated classrooms. He opposed homework on the grounds that the child had already expended a proper amount of time in learning in the school room.[53]

Those who criticized the public schools generally did so in reaction to sectarian factors as delineated in a previous chapter on religious controversy. Some minorities established or continued parochial schools to avoid both contaminated sectarian and secular education. Cincinnati, with its large number of Catholics, elected Catholic representatives to the school board, and methods of accommodation on the key issues of Bible reading and taxes were developed sooner there than in outlying areas. The *Catholic Telegraph,* nevertheless, criticized the common schools for lack of discipline, lack of uniform and effective instruction, irregular attendance, lack of parental interest, and lack of resources. The youth of America under this system showed "a mischievous precocity and refined depravity... which we look for in vain among the youth of pagan antiquity. Crimes, which in former days required the maturity of manhood to concoct and perpetuate, are committed by persons of both sexes hardly past the age of reason."[54]

Commitment to education among most Protestants included a lively interest in colleges. Friction developed in the case of the public colleges because the Presbyterians had a higher proportion of persons qualified to teach in them. They very often staffed and controlled colleges like Ohio and Miami Universities and these institutions were distinctly sectarian as a result.[55] The Presbyterians obviously did not mind having and holding their favored positions in these public institutions and they were probably correct in assuming that Methodists and others would have been equally satisfied had the preponderance of influence been with them.[56] Wise of the *Israelite* saw in this sectarian control of public universities "one of the most injurious evils of our country." Because of this unfortunate situation, he urged that a Jewish college be established to teach Jewish national literature. The college would be both piously Jewish and fully American and would unite the liberal principles with the American spirit.[57] Every religious faction similarly endeavored to nationalize itself in America, blending the sacred and the secular in education and using sectarian institutions to do so.

One of the most popular actions of the Jackson administration had been the removal of all Indian tribes to the west of the Mississippi River. Practically all Indian titles to lands east of the Mississippi had been liquidated by 1840. Regardless of its popularity, the policy was often callous and inhumane and these features aroused the conscience of editors until there was a significantly hostile reaction to Indian removal. The editor of the *Ohio Observer,* already cited as one of Jackson's bitter opponents, saw all sorts of fateful possibilities in Jackson's refusal to execute the decision of the Supreme Court by protecting the rights of the Cherokees to their lands in Georgia. These possibilities included the dissolution of the Union, the impeachment of Jackson, or the entire nullification of the Constitution. Cholera, however, proved to be the instrument of punishment. Its ravages indicated that the "judgements of Heaven are awake; nor should it be a matter of surprise. As a Nation we deserve to be scourged. We have outraged the laws of God and man."[58] The editor of the *Cincinnati Journal,* at one time accused of supporting Jackson, anticipated that the proposed removal would be but the first in a series of "removals" until either the Pacific was reached or the Indian was exterminated. "If the government is not disposed to deal equitably by the Indians on this side of the river, what security have they that justice will be dispensed to them on the other?" Georgians were no more selfish now than future residents west of the Mississippi would be later. "Indian rights and stipulated treaties, will ever prove feeble barriers against the encroachment of avarice, aided by power."[59]

Editors were not remiss in offering suggestions bearing upon a solution to the Indian problem. The Quaker *Philanthropist* urged human and reasonable attitudes on the part of both individuals and the government in helping the Indian adapt to a new mode of life. This help would come through advice, implements of agriculture, and examples by the white man in social, political, and religious obligation. A Presbyterian in Indiana urged that the Gospel itself be looked to for the energy to develop mechanical and agricultural skills among the Indians, thus making it possible to assimilate the Indian fully into the white man's way of life. But an Ohio Baptist despaired of a solution, for he doubted the government's ability to shield the Indian from the rapaciousness of the white man. Perhaps removal was the best policy but, if so, the philanthropic few must atone for the wrongs as much as possible by furnishing "the means and benefits of Christian and civil institutions."[60]

The most grievous questions in foreign policy for this class of editors involved England, except for the Mexican War. The physical encounter between Canadians and Americans in the *Caroline* and MacLeod affair, the Maine boundary dispute, and the searching of United States ships in the British effort to suppress the slave trade yielded to the diplomatic talents and mutual respect of Daniel Webster and Lord Ashburton in 1842. This development came as a great relief to editors of religious newspapers in the Northwest. War over any one or all of these issues they deemed repugnant, impolitic, dishonorable, and immoral. One editor declared that the ratification of the Webster-Ashburton Treaty was the event most worthy of celebration since the end of the War of 1812.[61] Editors proved themselves quite able to cope with the jingoism and the intricacies of party politics when the Democractic administration of James K. Polk negotiated the compromise which divided the Oregon Territory.[62]

Editors were at least vaguely committed to the moral philosophy and general objectives of the contemporary peace movement and gave extensive space to news of organized peace efforts. This commitment to peace was not in the form of absolute pacifism, nor did it apply to a moral issue such as slavery or any event involving the security of the nation. It was not unusual for an editor to claim that the inspiration of the peace movement had produced a strong moral sentiment which made such settlements possible.[63]

Editors of religious newspapers had occasion to weigh the pros and cons of intervention in Europe. The Hungarian Revolution received special attention among religious leaders because of the dramatic challenge to old world autocracy and Catholic domination and because of the subsequent visit of its leader, Louis Kossuth, to America in 1851-1852. With Protestants there was an instinctive sympathy for Hungary, and editors attempted to fill the gaps in their readers' knowledge of the nation and its people. Opinion on Kossuth and his visit was restrained and carefully qualified, however. In spite of their delight in Kossuth's anti-Catholic position, some Protestants were suspicious of a deistic strain in his religion. Editors were also fearful that the United States might be tempted from its tradition of nonintervention by Kossuth's visit.

The episode caused editors, for the most part, to define American obligation to the rest of the world in the usual terms of example and moral suasion rather than in terms of intervention. Some at least hinted at a latent interventionism, however. One editor, after decidedly declaring himself for nonintervention, thought that it might be necessary to engage in a "severe contest" if God's designs for liberty were thwarted by an attack on England by the despots of Europe. A Methodist realistically warned that the United States must be prepared to back up any "paper commitments" with force or "we shall be despicable." But his call was for the United States to prepare herself by building internal strength for the time when the despotism of Europe would inevitably try to reach further. A Baptist in Michigan wanted it understood that George Washington's nonintervention did not imply "indifferentism." A German Reformed personality accepted with calm resolve rumors of United States' naval preparations. War was a great evil but "we are glad if the result of it be the overthrow of that most perfidious of all human governments, the Austrian Empire."[64] The *Catholic Telegraph* resigned itself to the "Kossuth Mania," but the editor was so irked by the Hungarian's popularity that he wrote: "Twenty-three hours of the Day of Judgement will be taken up with Editors, Politicians, and Brokers" and one hour with all the rest of the population.[65]

Religious papers in the Northwest showed an unusual interest in the interventionism which opened the exotic lands of China and Japan. Editors hailed the T'ai P'ing rebellion in China in the 1850's partly because its leadership incorporated some Protestant doctrines into its ideology. But more significantly, a Methodist editor warned that "the white sails of the merchantman must be furled in every harbor, or the thunder of the man-of-war will be heard.... She [Japan] must quicken her pace or the round shot will overtake her." Much to his regret, this opening came at a time when the missionary treasury of the Methodist Church was empty. A Presbyterian could not refrain from pride in the fact that the forced opening of Japan had "secured an end which European diplomacy had vainly sought for more than two centuries."[66]

The theme of "manifest destiny" was lyrically expressed by a few editors. The redeeming of the Mississippi Valley from a "degenerate and less energetic race" had been accomplished by "hardy, aspiring and practical men" and the area of freedom extended almost involuntarily by the people of the United States. Only the "Idol of Manifest Destiny," not manifest destiny itself, could dishonor the nation. A Baptist could contemplate the moral results of territorial acquisitions and "the stupendous future almost with the glowing warmth of inspiration." The *Catholic Telegraph* reluctantly adjusted to Protestant America's conquest of a part of Mexico upon discovery that the action had not interfered with the Catholic Church there. Furthermore, since the Church in Cuba had been injured under existing conditions, a transfer of Cuba to the United States would allow for the cleansing of Cubans by the purer North American Catholicism. "Call it ambition, or land piracy, lust for conquest, or Anglo-Saxon unscrupulous avarice—or what you will—it is a determined fact that there is but one flag in the Northern half of the American continent," he wrote. Even the *Western Friend,* a Quaker weekly, chronicled America's expansion to include an "empire on the Pacific" with relish.[67]

One of the services of the religious newspaper was to give news and documents pertaining to state and local affairs, often in the form of separate columns appropriately labeled. It was normal to give the Governor's address to the legislature and a weekly summary of activity when the legislature was in session. Editors publicized reports from various state agencies, especially those dealing with the insane and the physically handicapped, giving universally enthusiastic approval for improvement in these services. It was not altogether rare for public servants, state or local, to be criticized by name. It was also apparent that politicians paid tribute to the influence of these editors by mailing them government documents and thoughtfully visiting their offices.

There was considerable range to editors' comments on items of purely local interest. One editor reminded his fellow townsmen of Circleville, Ohio, that his service to the community included a substantial expenditure of funds gathered from nonresidents, hence the justice in local citizens subscribing to his paper. An editor in Jacksonville, Illinois, chastised a grocer for favoritism to select customers by reserving choice cuts of meat for them.[68] Another editor complained that the tolls of the Zanesville-Bridgeport Road in Ohio were excessive, suggesting that "there is rather too much fingering of the people's money." Another was critical of the ostentatious reception accorded John Q. Adams when he came to Cincinnati. "A more republican mode of reception, and the absence of sham would better suit our views."[69]

Community improvement projects sometimes drew support. These included a plea for sidewalks and the improvement of the public square in Monmouth, Illinois. Rejected, on the other hand, was the suggestion that the streets of Cincinnati be cleaned at night for the convenience of her citizens. To require people to work at night was contrary to nature and dangerous to health, insisted a Presbyterian. He held steam power responsible for the increased pace of life requiring people to work under these strange circumstances. Another Cincinnati editor joined in support of the creation of a public park in Cincinnati and hoped it would be only the beginning of something better.[70]

Religious papers were consistently vocal in the area of public health and safety. They encouraged vaccination programs, a more professional approach to medicine, and co-operation with local authorities in controlling diseases such as rabies. One editor warned of the potential for severe injury to arms thrust out the windows of the omnibuses, new in Cincinnati in 1849, because of the dangerous arrangement of their rear wheels.[71] One young lady had suffocated in a privy vault when the floor gave way and another person had been stuck for two hours in a less serious accident. Surely this was sufficient warning to build the floors of privies so that they might be safe.[72]

It is clear that there was no complete or permanent barrier in religious newspapers to editorializing on public policies, even those which involved political action. Far the most overtly political writing on the editorial pages, however, was to deal with slavery and sooner or later practically all Protestant editors were recommending specific political action on that subject. The fact that many editors had already crossed that boundary on other issues made the step easier with slavery. But more than any other issue, slavery was so compelling morally that it must be engaged politically by those who were commissioned of God to instruct the world in righteousness.

Chapter VI
THE POLITICS OF SLAVERY

The Old Northwest was the scene of some of the most significant events in the moral and political crusade against slavery. It was in Ohio that Theodore Dwight Weld's antislavery regiments formed in the 1830's after the rebellion at Lane Seminary in Cincinnati.[1] Alton, Illinois, was the scene of one of the dramatic moments in abolition history with the martyrdom of Elijah Lovejoy in 1837. The region furnished its share and more of the signers of antislavery petitions praying the Congress to abolish slavery in Washington, D.C., and in the territories and to stop the domestic slave trade. From this area came an increasing number of politicians serving on the national front against slavery, including Salmon P. Chase, Joshua Giddings, Edward and Benjamin Wade, and Zachariah Chandler. Above all, the Northwest gave spontaneous birth to the Republican party. The votes of Ohio, Michigan, and Wisconsin went to Republican John C. Frémont in 1856 and all five states went for native son, Abraham Lincoln, in 1860. This result represented in no small way the moral and political triumph of those who had registered the antislavery impulse in the 1830's.[2]

The conductors of religious journals in the Northwest rendered effective support for the antislavery cause. Although most of them were critical of abolitionists, they eventually adopted some of their methods which included intense agitation, the use of petitions, and the support of antislavery parties in politics. Editors were moved by moral earnestness born of religious conviction which was at least as efficient in the turmoil of the editorial office as in the pentecostal flame of the revival that has received so much scholarly attention. The political sentiment which this morality inspired was finally registered editorially in favor of the Republican party by nearly all Protestant editors.

The only papers of consequence in the Northwest before 1825 were the Presbyterian *Weekly Recorder* and the
Quaker *Philanthropist* and both were antislavery. They
objected to the Missouri Compromise on the basis that
Missouri's pro-slavery constitution allowed slavery to expand beyond its original boundaries. According to the
Recorder, the progress of slavery "should be arrested,
and means should be adopted for its speedy and gradual
abolition—for its utter extinction." Elisha Bates, who
acquired the *Philanthropist* from the abolitionists, Benjamin Lundy and Charles Osborn, often expressed his
abhorrence of slavery. He admitted colonization arguments into his columns only because "every investigation
of the subject will tend to open the eyes." Otherwise he
questioned the practicability of colonization on the
grounds that the Negro did not want it and that slavery
produced too much ignorance and vice to qualify the
Negro to evangelize Africa. One's position on colonization was to be a major test of one variety of abolitionist.
The Garrison and Weld groups rejected colonization
while nearly all editors of religious newspapers continued
to support it at least mildly to 1860.[3]

As the antislavery movements evolved, those clergymen with the more radical views tended to "come out,"
forming such groups as the Wesleyan Methodists, Free
Presbyterians, American Reformed Tract and Book Society, and Oberlin College. Therefore, generally moderate
sentiment was left in control of most editorial chairs. As
members of the most radical groups, the staff at Oberlin
attended local and national antislavery meetings and,
through the *Evangelist,* promoted them. The paper supported such Ohio politicians as the Wades and Giddings
and correctly forecast their future for having "consulted
the true interests of the people." Staff members participated in the Lorain County Antislavery Society meeting which pledged its members not to vote for any candidate to Congress who was not in favor of the immediate

abolition of slavery in the District of Columbia and in the territories, and for prohibition of the internal slave trade. They not only protested colonization but they urged the return of suffering émigrés from Liberia to the United States.[4]

Elijah Lovejoy of the *Alton Observer* did not actually "come out," but he did complain because the New School Presbyterians did not separate themselves from the pro-slavery Old School in 1837, a division postponed for two years. Lovejoy had helped to organize the Illinois Antislavery Society and had circulated the usual abolitionist petitions. Lovejoy's paper was a rather conventional Presbyterian newspaper and in his infrequent editorials on slavery he was less extreme than some of his fellow journalists to the East. He approved colonization as a missionary device so long as it was not proposed as a remedy for slavery or as a condition of emancipation. Lovejoy's last editorial was entitled "Fault Finders" and was directed toward those who were more critical of reformers than they were of wrongdoers.[5]

Lovejoy's death, which occurred at Alton, Illinois, November 7, 1837, as he was defending his press against destruction by a mob, caused much commotion among his colleagues. During some of his earlier troubles, the famous Baptist leader, John Mason Peck, of nearby Rock Springs, wrote of Lovejoy's editorials as "sparks thrown into a powder magazine." He specifically criticized Lovejoy's "fanatical" suggestion for hanging some "mobites" who had attacked an abolitionist in Michigan. Peck implied that Lovejoy should not have been surprised at being the object of retaliation for such extreme statements.[6] He remained silent after Lovejoy's death until the *Cincinnati Journal* published a letter from Alton accusing Peck of basing his silence on his desire to remain popular. Peck then carried a seven-column article on fanaticism early in 1838 without any mention of Lovejoy. A few weeks later he pleaded for understanding: "A very few persons, from either not perceiving our fixed purpose formed at the earliest stage, to stand aloof from the peculiar excitements of others around us, which have resulted in violence and death... may have misapprehended our course."[7] Peck had some credentials of his own in moderately antislavery activity, having participated in the founding of the Illinois Antislavery League in the 1820's. He did not, however, believe that the problem of slavery could be resolved by agitation in religious circles.[8]

The martyrdom of Lovejoy also placed a strain on a similarly mild Baptist in Ohio, Noble S. Johnson, of the *Cross and Journal.* He was a colonizationist who was outspoken enough to be accused by the *Cincinnati Gazette* of being "half or more an abolitionist." Johnson accepted this as an insult and decided not to discuss abolition in his paper, but he especially emphasized that he would not criticize it. When Johnson recorded the destruction of Lovejoy's first press in Alton he had denounced the mob and warned that such conduct increased the attractiveness of abolition. Nevertheless, he made the central issue in the Lovejoy killing the sacredness of a free press rather than slavery.[9]

Elisha W. Chester, editor of the Presbyterian *Journal* in Cincinnati, enclosed his front page in black when he described the "Horrid Tragedy" of Lovejoy's death. He also tried unsuccessfully to continue the *Observer* by printing it in Cincinnati for shipment to Alton. The New School *Journal* had moderately opposed slavery for a decade, but its former editors had firmly supported colonization and voiced objection to much of the emphasis of the antislavery societies. They had repudiated the abolitionism of the Englishman George Thompson and of William Lloyd Garrison because "it assumes that all slaveholders are felons, and heaps upon them unmeasured denunciations." In the crisis induced by antislavery activity at Lane Seminary, the staff of the *Journal* reversed its early sympathy for the rebels, scolding them for claiming unique moral excellence and for asserting their youth and inexperience against the wisdom of their elders.[10]

Lovejoy's death prompted the editor of the *Ohio Observer* to write that "the deed of horror, so long and unblushingly threatened, is done. The voice of blood, and the cry of justice, ... call us to awake to the signs of the times." This paper, through a succession of editors, had repudiated slavery as "that blackest and most heinous" of sins. Its editors, on the other hand, could see no incompatibility between abolitionism and colonization. Nor did they concede that abolitionists had "all the conscience, integrity of purpose, all the moral and intellectual light, and all the high moral courage in the country."[11]

Aside from the impact of Lovejoy's death, the strong moral tone of the abolition crusade forced editors and their churches to align themselves with regard to it during the 1830's. The United Brethren removed William Rhinehart and installed William Hanby, a shift from an ardent abolitionist to a moderate antislavery man. At the same time authorities of the church imposed restrictions upon discussion of slavery in the *Telescope* in the interest of denominational unity, a policy which was not formally rescinded until 1845. Hanby had opposed slavery but he pledged to do so "with due deference to the feelings of the pious and good." He opposed the Garrison school, as did many others, because of Garrison's denunciation of the churches.[12]

The Methodist family of papers was also distinctly hostile toward abolitionism thus following the lead of denominational executives.[13] The abolitionists were men "who with entire recklessness of consequences, seem resolved on *emancipation and amalgamation*," a remedy worse than the disease. But there were contrary signs. Charles Elliott, who became editor of the *Western Chris-*

tian Advocate in 1836, was very critical of the gag rule in the House of Representatives and he warned that if the people were made to choose between the loss of the right of petition and abolitionism, they would choose the latter.[14] Elliott featured his platform on slavery in the first issue of the new volume after the General Conference in 1840, when the denomination was already experiencing the throes of the division which materialized four years later. The Conference had asked him not to agitate the issue in the church during the quadrennium. Fortunately, wrote Elliott, they had not enjoined him or he would have refused the post. He protected himself somewhat from the potential wrath of his superiors by listing the sins of the abolitionists. They promoted a schismatic spirit, they tended to be political revolutionaries, they generally sacrificed piety for zeal, their effect on slaves was pernicious because of the unrealistic expectations they aroused, and they had denounced and misrepresented the United States abroad.[15] A Methodist Protestant clergyman also identified himself with "abolition conservatism." A conservative was one who held two or more ideas but who would oppose slavery in any form, would favor emancipation in any way consistent with duty to his church and the state, would not bend his will to the fanatic, and would resent the ambitious few who capitalized on the antislavery sentiment.[16]

Episcopal, Universalist, and Catholic papers contained little on slavery and what they did contain was critical of the agitation. The Episcopal editor was satisfied to advance "vital and practical religion" as the means to produce an indirect effect for good relative to slavery. Universalists despised the hatred fomented between the North and South, especially in anticipation of an expansion of the Universalist ministry into the South. The *Catholic Telegraph* urged the *status quo* as the lesser of two evils, at least until some gradual remedy for slavery became available. Slavery was so grave an evil that "the power is not equal to the will of putting an end to it."[17] All these groups remained consistent with these views during the next two decades and did not figure largely in the debate.

In its next phase the antislavery movements generated first the Liberty Party of 1840 and 1844, then the Free Soil party of 1848 and 1852. Although the Free Soil party was involved in the complexity of broader political rivalries, it did provide the focal point for the growing influence of antislavery sentiment in politics and helped to prepare the stage for the rise of the Republican party as a major power in the Northwest in 1854. The expansion of the nation to the Pacific during these years intensified the antislavery emotions and gave them increasingly sharp political focus on the principle of containment. Most key Protestant journals published during these twelve years, each in its own style, endorsed the Wilmot Proviso, opposed the Compromise of 1850 in principle and the specific provisions which might allow slavery to expand, and they were particularly bitter toward the Fugitive Slave Law.[18]

The *Oberlin Evangelist* was the most emphatic in its political alignment. It gave as the best of the alternatives before the voter in 1840 "the 'Liberty Ticket,' of the noble [James G.] Birney and [Thomas] Earle" and registered the same party sentiment with slightly less emphasis in 1844. The opposition of the *Evangelist* to the Mexican War was so fierce that it forbade joy at its end.[19] The editor of the *Evangelist* was one of the most fervent delegates at the Buffalo Free Soil Convention which nominated Martin Van Buren in 1848. His only disappointment was the narrowness of Van Buren's nonextension views though he still rejoiced that this much principle could be achieved in a political movement. By the *Evangelist's* private decree, the Fugitive Slave Law was declared unconstitutional, although the editor counseled the fugitives not to resist it with violence. The *Evangelist* in 1852 endorsed the candidate of the fading Free Soil party, John P. Hale, pleading for the political unification of the free soil and abolition factions.[20].

The Plan of Union *Western Herald* announced as an antislavery paper in 1846, although its editor, James B. Walker, did not advocate the immediate expulsion of slaveholders from the churches and he supported the prosecution of the war with Mexico "now we have it on our hands." He gave extensive coverage to the Free Soil Convention in Buffalo in the expectation that its principles would eventually prevail whether or not its candidate did in 1848. Walker asked his readers whether they would want their vote in the presidential election to come under scrutiny at the Judgment Day. This unique form of pressure seems to confirm his interest in the Free Soil party as did his hailing with "so much pleasure" the election of Chase in far-off Ohio.[21]

Supported extensively by its constituent presbyteries and synods, the *Watchman of the Valley* in Cincinnati became more and more an advocate of the free soil position in politics. When the editor discussed Van Buren's nomination in 1848 he carried an additional four columns relating activities of free soil groups. He gave an unequivocal endorsement of Van Buren on the eve of the election, though he did not expect him to win.[22] In 1849 T.A. Mills became editor of this paper, henceforth called the *Central Christian Herald*. Mills expected his readers to call upon "God to avert from the free territories ... the curse of slavery.... Our sympathies on this subject we cannot doubt, are in unison with God's." The issue was completely outside any category where the Compromise of 1850 could be appropriate, and Senator William H. Seward's "Higher Law" speech rejecting the Compromise was an expression of "true moral heroism." Mills advised that a Christian might disobey the Fugitive Slave Law "and pay the penalty, whatever it might be," if he did not resist violently. The relative quiet of free soil forces in 1852, he warned, did not imply that they would be satisfied until slavery ceased to exist.[23]

The Methodist *Advocate* in Cincinnati was one of the most significant examples of the steady shift toward overt political involvement. Some of Elliott's inhibitions in discussing slavery lifted after the division of Methodism in 1844 and after a jury in Parkersburg, Virginia, condemned his paper as incendiary. He wrote kindly of the Liberty party in 1846 and thereafter editorialized frequently on the moral and political evil in the further extension of slavery. Matthew Simpson isolated in the election of 1848 "a single question of moral bearing . . . *the extension of slavery.*" The day for action was fast approaching when every man would be "compelled to show his position" and the result would be the realignment of parties. After conditional approval of the Compromise, Simpson reacted to the Fugitive Slave Law in "utter astonishment that such a law could have been passed in any enlightened tribunal."[24]

The *Watchman of the Prairies* in Chicago, which was to be the base for the strongest Baptist paper in the Northwest, deplored the Mexican War. In one sentence the editor rejected the Whig and Democratic nominees in 1848: "In General Taylor the Nation will have a Southern man with Southern principles, while in General Cass we have a Northern man with Southern principles." He praised the Buffalo Free Soil Convention for breaking "the trammels of party" and providing a place for the morally committed. He received Daniel Webster's Seventh of March Speech in support of the Compromise of 1850 "with mingled astonishment and regret," but Seward's speech was "of a different character. It makes no compromise with what is right, but moves straight forward with cleanness and power."[25]

The Baptist paper in Ohio illustrated the problem for moral and intellectual statesmanship when dealing with slavery in this era. The moderate George Cole offered a series of editorials in the *Cross and Journal* November 26, 1846, to March 12, 1847, in which he analyzed slavery with all its ramifications. "The question is," he wrote, "what shall we do, things being as they are, not as they ought to be?" Cole traced the sin and guilt involved in slavery back to the slave trade and into much of the North's own economic system. Even so, the South was wrong in asking to be relieved of the criticism of its cherished system which all good men must aggressively challenge. But, since the whole nation shared in the guilt, denunciation of the South was not appropriate and would not resolve the problem. The most practical step which Cole could suggest was that a group of prominent citizens from the South who could admit that slavery was wrong, and a similar group from the North who could accept slaveholders as Christians, meet in convention to draw up a plan for gradual, compensated emancipation, entailing the sacrifice of all citizens. "If slavery is ever abolished short of revolution and bloodshed we believe that those who are willing to make some sacrifices will have the honor of the deed." Cole received almost equal abuse from his northern constituents and from his Baptist colleagues in the South.[26]

Upon being relieved of the denominationally imposed curbs in discussing slavery, the United Brethren *Religious Telescope* condemned the annexation of Texas and the Mexican War. Its editor declared in 1846 that "political abolitionism" was outside the legitimate concern of his paper, but he did write that "the Liberty party is destined at no distant day to be a great and leading party." By 1852 the *Telescope* saw in Hale the chosen of God "to shake the stagnant elements of political and moral death which have been settling upon our beloved country."[27]

Conservative editors, in addition to those previously mentioned, changed their positions very little from 1840-1852. The Methodist Protestant *Recorder* shot editorial bolts at slavery but refused an endorsement since no party could be free of the "managers of the wires." Among German Lutherans, the Wittenberg Synod in Ohio did label slavery a national disgrace but the Joint Synod was more moderate and neither the English nor the German papers became involved in the politics of slavery. The German Reformed press was similarly silent in the Northwest and was rarely vocal elsewhere before the Civil War. The Old School *Presbyterian of the West* was critical of those who fought bondage to slavery instead of bondage to sin. The editor objected to attacks on the Fugitive Slave Law, regretting that it gave cause both for some legitimate grief and for the raving of fanatics.[28]

The passage of the Kansas-Nebraska Bill in 1854 completed the process of converting most denominational papers into political organs. Those which had already endorsed antislavery third parties or their platforms were even more solidly and enthusiastically Republican because of the larger prospects of success and because the coalescence of a major political party around the issue of slavery had been the object of editors' prayers for years. Some papers made significant shifts from opposition to support for antislavery politics. This identification of Protestant newspapers with the Republican party is the overwhelming fact, in this medium of communication, during this decade. Reactions of editors to other major events in the conflict between the North and South 1854-1861 were predictable and these incidents only served to consolidate existing political alignments.

The reaction in the Northwest to the proposed Kansas-Nebraska Bill was immediate and savage with the severest reactions occurring among the constituents of the author, Stephen Douglas, in Chicago. The clergy there attempted to duplicate the efforts of the New England and New York clergy in petitioning Congress in opposition to the bill. Antislavery politicians such as Seward had long recognized the appeal of the higher law doctrine, had campaigned with the evangelical clergy in mind, and had openly cultivated religious groups. A statement reportedly made by Seward to a Methodist conference to the effect that he was an Episcopalian in religion and a Methodist in politics corresponded to reality.[29] Senators Salmon Chase and Charles Sumner also recognized the value of clerical support in the battle against the Kansas-Nebraska Bill and expressly solicited the support of the clergy and their organizations as petition mechanisms.[30]

Twenty-five Chicago area clergymen[31] signed the resolutions of protest and they gathered about 500 supporting signatures from other clergy in the Northwest in a brief campaign. Of the major Protestant papers in Chicago at that time, the only one not represented at the meeting was the Baptist *Christian Times,* which subsequently supported the petition. Douglas responded in the Senate and in a letter addressed to the Chicago clergy. He objected to their claim that the clergy was divinely appointed to declare and enforce "God's will upon all points of moral and religious truth" whether or not the points had a political bearing. This, Douglas declared, was "subversive of the principles of free government, and destructive of all the guarantees of civil and religious liberty." The argument, never very enlightening on either side, continued over whether, in their original form, the resolutions had the ministers speaking "in the name of Almighty God."[32]

The two most vociferous editors on this occasion were the Congregational and the Methodist. The editor of the *Congregational Herald* labeled Douglas "our treacherous Senator," whom he contrasted with the faithful Chase, Seward, and Sumner. The paper accused Douglas of lying about the wording of the protest and threatened his political future for his attack upon the clergy. Watson, editor of the largest paper of any type in the city, the *Northwestern Christian Advocate,* had been one of the chief authors of the protest. It took more than five columns to contain his reply to Douglas' letter. He denied that it was contrary to the principle of the separation of church and state to do as the clergy had done. Politicians must submit to the rebuke of ministers who were responsible for the interests of society at the highest level. Ministers must "specify the immorality of a political measure."[33]

The religious newspapers eagerly observed and chronicled the public rallies in protest of the Kansas-Nebraska Bill and the discernible shape of a new political party. Having learned more of political expediency by this time, the staff of the *Oberlin Evangelist* advocated the election of local and national Republican candidates in 1856 and gave all party activities extensive publicity. The results, however, did show that no party could "rule in righteousness" until it more completely "embraced the doctrine of equal rights for all mankind." The *Evangelist* came out for Lincoln in 1860, rejecting the view that it was "morally wrong to vote for a second best man—it being supposed that he is the best man who can be elected." The results of the election in this case seemed "an indication that God has not forsaken us."[34]

The *Congregational Herald* expressed pride in the clergy's role in mobilizing opinion for Frémont in 1856. The paper showed the usual mixed feelings of radicals toward Lincoln in 1858 during the course of his debates with Douglas. By convention time in 1860, however, the *Herald* was willing to concede that the Republican platform and candidate represented the outer boundary of public opinion. After the election, the editor congratulated his readers upon the triumph of freedom: "Our hearts are jubilant, our lips overflow with praise to God. As Christians we rejoice at the auspicious result of the portentous struggle, even as Christians we labored and prayed to secure it."[35]

A New School Presbyterian believed that the hated

Kansas-Nebraska Bill would do more to overthrow slavery than a decade of abolitionist activities had been able to do. The 1856 election became for this editor the most important election in America's history. He could not conscientiously use his candidate's name, but he could urge his readers to vote in the fear of God. In spite of the Republican failure in 1856, it was his firm conviction that the election had settled permanently the question of the further extension of slavery.[36]

The editor of the *Ohio Observer* had not been able to suppress his Whig leanings sufficiently to affiliate with the Free Soil party in 1848 although he was absolutely opposed to the extension of slavery. In 1854, however, the action of Congress convinced him that the North must use its numerical strength in politics to resist the further spread of slavery *"upon any consideration whatsoever!"* He then urged ministers to use the machinery of the church to petition Congress. The success of the anti-Nebraska faction in 1854 gave the editor "more courage and confidence" in the validity of free institutions than he had ever had before.[37]

The Old School *Presbyterian of the West* made one of the more dramatic shifts to free soil politics. The paper in 1854, during a transfer of ownership to Joseph Montfort, opposed the Kansas-Nebraska Bill in principle, and then defended the anti-Nebraska party in politics. Montfort wondered whether one would apply popular sovereignty to polygamy or to the death penalty. He thus persuaded himself to challenge any introduction of slavery into territories previously free and "the more we do battle every day," he wrote, "the better we rest at night." Unlike some, he did not feel that the election of Douglas would automatically preclude further resistance to the spread of slavery.[38] The United Presbyterian publication in Monmouth, Illinois, was also tolerant of other political elements while leaning toward Republican doctrines and vocabulary, i.e., nonextension of slavery, a free press, and free speech.[39]

The two Methodist Episcopal papers gave unequivocal support to the Republicans from the first. They were fully supported in their antislavery politics by the resolutions of constituent conferences except for southern sections of Illinois and Indiana.[40] Elliott in Cincinnati urged men to overlook previous party affiliation and to join the new antislavery party to "promote, by political action, the good of the country." He rejoiced in the progress made by antislavery elements in the elections of 1854 "as a work of principle and moral power." In an editorial he called "The Crisis," Elliott analyzed the choice before the voters in 1856 after he had strengthened the voters' will with inflammatory reports of the violence in Kansas. Elliott's successor, Calvin Kingsley, criticized President James Buchanan's advocacy of the Lecompton Constitution and rejoiced "most devoutly" when the "stupendous fraud" was eventually rebuked by Congress. During the campaign of 1860, however, he confined himself to defending the Republicans from charges that they would interfere with slavery in the South and charges that Methodist editors were leaders among Black Republicans.[41]

Watson in Chicago enthusiastically followed the mass meetings which gave birth to the Republican party, announcing after the one in Jackson, Michigan: "Our politics are—the Alpha and Omega of the politics of the *Northwestern* are—that every Christian should be found at the polls, going anti-whiskey and anti-Nebraska." After the fall election in 1854 he commented: "It is with unfeigned gratitude to an oppression-hating God, that we find ourselves permitted to record the complete triumph of the 'anti-Nebraska and Kansas bill' doctrines ... in the great states of Indiana, Ohio, and Pennsylvania ... Our rejoicing over this fact is not political, it is Christian." His last editorial prior to his death urged his readers to go from their "closets to the polls. Trust in God and vote in His fear."[42]

In 1858, Watson's successor, T.M. Eddy, from southern Indiana, delivered a sermon at a camp meeting in White Pigeon, Michigan, after which a local newspaper denounced him as a "Black Republican Reverend." The incident netted Eddy shouts of praise and admiration from Michigan Methodists plus a "well deserved" 500 new subscribers from the conference. By 1859 he was urging his readers to participate in the crucial nominating process of the parties as the only means of elevating the proper men to office. His delight in the large attendance at Republican rallies in 1860 as well as his displeasure at the "proslavery" electioneering of Peter Cartwright, a loyal Democrat who supported Douglas, left no doubt as to his position.[43]

The German Methodist paper was also openly Republican. Editor Nast himself attended anti-Nebraska meetings and denounced the Kansas-Nebraska Bill in public and in print. In 1856 he indicated his conviction that political neutrality was no longer possible and in 1860 he gave his endorsement to the political revolution which was bearing its full fruit in the election.[44]

Two of three important Baptist papers supported the position of the Republican party. The third, the *Journal and Messenger,* identified slavery as the all-absorbing issue in 1856 and rather pointedly used the key phrases of the Republican platform in editorials but avoided a call to political action. The *Christian Times* of Chicago supported free soil and free speech in 1856 and called upon the religious press and the pulpit to get involved in behalf of the success of that doctrine. The representatives of the Republican party "made a demonstration very flattering to themselves" in the Chicago convention of 1860, while the Democratic convention was "a scene of violence and strife in striking contrast." There was nothing "invidious" intended in this unflattering contrast. The Baptist paper in Michigan showed much the same interest in Republican activities from the beginning. When Lincoln's election was finally assured, the editor acclaimed the result and naively forecast peace and good feeling to follow.[45]

Editors of United Brethren and Evangelical papers were coy, but they gave their readers an abundance of clues as to how they should vote in 1856 and 1860. The *Religious Telescope* viewed all politicians as unreliable but found it natural to dissent from Senator Douglas and President Franklin Pierce. By the same token, "if any other party takes a position more in accordance with the Christian doctrine of universal brotherhood, the *Telescope* will appear to favor that party." In 1860, Lawrence praised the Republican convention and its works though he was still disappointed with the failure of party politicians to defend adequately the rights of the Negro. The Evangelical papers voiced bitter reaction to the Kansas-Nebraska Bill but avoided expression of overt party sympathy.[46]

The Scandinavian papers in Illinois and Wisconsin began typically on the Democratic side in politics in the 1850's but changed to Republican during the decade. The Swedish *Hemlandet,* in 1855, pointedly labeled the Democratic party as the party of slavery and, in a special issue in 1856, committed the paper to the Republican party. This position was based on "a firm conviction received partly from the Word of God, confirmed by some knowledge of American History and existing conditions." The editor's support for Lincoln in his contest with Douglas in 1858 was total. The Norwegian *Kirke-Tidende* made the same shift for the same reasons.[47]

There were editors in addition to those previously described who assumed or continued either a neutral or a critical attitude toward antislavery politics.[48] The Episcopal *Chicago Record* had pursued a neutral policy during its brief antebellum history although its editor, James G. Wilson, must have repressed much feeling to accomplish this. He wrote thus after the 1860 election: "We thought it looked so well that our Church was the National Church.... And on this account, for pride's sake, a thousand Northern pulpits were silent on the subject of slavery, and men whose hearts ached to testify at the altar of God against its enormities, held their tongues and were still.'' The sad result was that the Episcopal clergy of the South had led the section in their treason.[49]

Benjamin Franklin of the *American Christian Review* consistently refused to state his position on slavery except to protest "one ideaism" and schism in the church. His Lord and the disciples had not given their position on slavery and neither would he. The Constitution in politics and the Bible in religion should be unqualifiedly obeyed. "Union under the Constitution given you by Providence, is your highest duty to God."[50] John Boggs edited a distinctly antislavery but weak paper as the only such organ among the Disciples. The few extant issues show its antislavery character but do not reveal its politics.[51]

The editor of the *Catholic Telegraph* was pleased that Catholics had refused to be a part of the political excitement engendered by slavery. The threatened division of the nation in 1860 was unfortunate but natural in a Protestant country. "The Northern Puritan, who cannot exist without annoying and persecuting somebody, has been sticking pins in the Southern people so long that they can endure it no more." The North, intolerant in both politics and religion, maintained "the right to a free Bible, free talking, free killing, and free booters." The German Catholic *Wahrheitsfreund* was clearly favorable to James Buchanan as "the most outstanding candidate" in 1856.[52]

Isaac Wise of the *Israelite* did not discuss the issue of slavery in his columns, but he may have been exceptional among Jews in the North in his silence and in his intense dislike of abolitionism.[53] His comment after the election of 1860 was: "The people of the United States just committed one of the greatest blunders a nation can commit, for which we must pay at once: They permitted extreme factions to play the hazardous game of the country's welfare and peace for an abstract idea." Wise considered the issue of slavery irrelevant and the Republican party's commitment to the Union insincere.[54]

Among those editors who had never subscribed to antislavery politics, even the most conservative eventually supported the Union cause or at least ceased to criticize it. This last was true of the *American Christian Review* but not before its circulation was seriously affected. Wise of the *Israelite,* after calling for a Messiah in the shape of an Oliver Cromwell to disband Congress and act against both extremes, pledged himself to total silence on the issue and the War and he honored his pledge[55] These two cases were isolated. Both German Reformed and German Lutheran editors in Ohio insisted that the conflict was originally unnecessary. Obedience to civil authority was, however, the duty of every citizen regardless of the nature of the cause.[56] The Universalist *Star in the West* called·upon its readers to dismiss all past reservations and to sustain the government at all costs. Later the editor declared accurately for all Universalist papers in the West, that they stood "unconditionally and uncompromisingly for the Union and for the country."[57]

Once the editor of the Episcopal *Record* in Chicago was released from his inhibitions, he became one of the most emotional Union supporters. The move by the North to vindicate freedom and outraged law was "a sublime and marvelous sight.... Five hundred thousand men are ready now for the contest with Treason.... Let the victory be complete, terrible, and overwhelming," he wrote in May, 1861. Bishop Charles P. McIlvaine used the *Western Episcopalian* to call upon the denomination to sustain fully the government, a duty which should be discharged zealously and sacrificially.[58]

The *Catholic Telegraph* reiterated its belief that the South had been imposed upon but the editor advised "fervent cooperation" with the government nevertheless.

The flag was threatened and Catholics must once more prove their devotion to the nation. Whatever his original sympathies, he explained, he could not endorse the caprice of the South in tearing down the national structure.[59]

All editors among those who indicated active support for the containment principle in politics gave their immediate and unqualified support to the Lincoln administration as civil war came. Most were realistic from the outset about the length and severity of the War and quickly sensed that it would bring an end to slavery. They uniformly and ardently believed that the South's attachment to slavery and her aggressiveness in extending it had brought on the War, leaving the Union Government no choice but to act to put down the rebellion. None seriously suggested compromise with the South to prevent secession. Editors varied in their early judgment of Lincoln's personality, ability, and his course of action but they were as one in rallying behind his decisions. The President was to have no more loyal support than that which he received from the editors of religious newspapers in the Old Northwest.

A large volume of recent scholarship has exposed the fact that northern zeal in opposition to slavery did not necessarily arise from or translate into zeal for racial equality. Free Negroes in the North were discriminated against in political rights, jobs, public accommodations, education, and access to public lands,[60] even though they were much freer to organize and speak out in their own behalf and to advance their interests in the courts than in the South. None of the editors of religious newspapers in the Old Northwest could escape the charge of racism when judged by absolute standards. Few, if any, believed without qualification that people of color could or should advance in status to a position of equality in every respect with white persons. There were numerous examples of the marks of racist consciousness. There was distress at the thought of the further concentration of poor and alleged crime-ridden Blacks in Cincinnati. There was negative reaction to the integration of Blacks into white congregations. Some editors believed that it was not right to promote among Blacks vain hopes of political and social equality. For a variety of stated reasons, the majority of Protestant editors supported voluntary colonization of Blacks outside the United States, even as their political actions against slavery increased. They generally accepted the view, whether or not they agreed with the sentiment upon which it was based, that prejudice was so deep that the Negro, regardless of his merit, could never achieve a full measure of freedom and equality in the United States.[61] But there was significant qualification of such views among these editors.

Even in the absence of extensive and more or less scientific studies to which the scholar now has access, some of the editors grappled with the issue of prejudice in relation to the actual condition of Blacks, both slave and free. "There is also a deep prejudice—silly, heartless, and often inhuman and wicked, it is true, but still deep seated—which chills and represses the spirit of the colored man," wrote a Michigan Baptist. "Flagrant and fatal injustice is often done to colored persons who may chance to travel by the various modes of conveyance owing to a silly and brainless prejudice against having such in the same car."[62] According to an Ohio Baptist, Blacks were totally deprived of "rights which reason and revelation both teach belong to *man* as *man*." One of the marks of man's depravity was "an antipathy, verging on an unnatural hatred, against the African race."[63] A Presbyterian opposed the view that prejudice against people of color was inborn and ineradicable. "The existence of this prejudice, ... we are ready to admit; but we regard it as moral rather than physical—acquired and not innate."[64] Another Presbyterian more profoundly and more realistically than most of his generation analyzed the interactions which intensified prejudice.

> The prejudices of the black men were bitter because those of the white men were inveterate. The one demands the equal rights of a common nature and the other refuses to *listen* to the claim. He will not admit him to his table, or his parlor, he will not permit their children to intermarry, he will not employ him as a lawyer or physician, nor elect him to posts of honor or emolument, and consequently there is a sense of injustice, and a feeling of unkindness, and these feelings react from one class to the other until the prejudice becomes as bitter on one side as it is supposed to be unreasonable on the other.

The same man saw an indication of a truly human spirit in rebelliousness among slaves considering it entirely natural for a slave to attempt to forcibly arise and gain a notion of his own power.[65] Some condescension may have been implied, but there was also some degree of liberality in editors' greeting the appearance of black leaders in convention, on the lecture platform, and in publishing activities as proof of what colored men not only could do but would increasingly be doing.[66]

Methodists, Baptists, Presbyterians, and Congregationalists were sharply critical of the liabilities imposed on free Blacks through the "Black Laws" of their states. These laws usually involved one or more of the following: efforts to discourage residence of Blacks in their states, restrictions on attendance of black children in public schools, restrictions on voting rights, segregation in public accommodations, and refusal to accept the testimony of Negroes against Whites in the courts. Editors typically denounced these laws in emotional language and chastised the voters and legislators for perpetuating them. In Illinois, a Methodist wrote that the Black Law of that state, "out Herods Herod, outdistances Draco." His fellow Methodist in Cincinnati angrily wrote that the Black Laws of Ohio "are a disgrace to the statute-book of any civilized country," when the legislature refused to repeal them. An Illinois Baptist called the action in Illinois "stupid," and the Chicago Baptist Association beheld it with "astonishment and horror," resolving to treat the discriminatory law as null and void.[67] A Presbyterian challenged the white residents of Ohio to relieve the Blacks of these liabilities and "if he is naturally inferior, as is claimed, then nothing is to be feared from competition with him." The editor of the *Oberlin Evangelist* grieved at the rejection of petitions for the repeal of Ohio's Black Laws. He criticized the politicians for again temporizing over the granting of "simple justice to men irrespective of their color—they cannot treat men as *men* . . . , they must have some disabilities founded solely on color of the skin."[68]

These reactions represent a relatively progressive attitude and insights well beyond those prevailing in the general population. They reflect changing perceptions based upon the implications of the inherited doctrine of natural rights and direct observation of concrete practices which were not consistent with that doctrine or the notion of the personhood of the Blacks before God. One can only speculate as to how much their scoldings may have encouraged the growth of these more positive attitudes among their readers.

EPILOGUE

The men who provided the far-reaching services of the religious newspaper responded to the challenges of an expanding and tumultuous society with dedication, energy, and courage. Their personal sacrifice in coin and convenience was too large and too consistent to allow for popular or academic cynicism. They persisted in showing individual facets of personality and viewpoint even when they effectively balanced their own tastes with the need to bring cohesion among a people of a varied economic, social, and intellectual state of being. Most of them were evangelical Protestants, which suggests an overwhelming interest in salvation now and in the world to come. But the symbolism of a newspaper containing intense promotion of religious conversion and denominational development side by side with bank-note tables and political speeches is unmistakable. They confidently presented to their fellows the best of two worlds, which men in other environments have often found incompatible. The sanctification of the secular, not its repudiation, was their goal, and this desire took editors deeply into the everyday affairs, public and private, of the people of the Old Northwest.

They confronted the inevitable stresses in the rapid mixing of people of diverse nationalities and religious beliefs already conditioned by severe, historical antagonisms. Twentieth-century spokesmen, in spite of their own dismal record, have often approached the social and religious conflicts of antebellum America with terms which, in themselves, imply censure. Nineteenth-century disputants were often tarnished by rank bigotry, which then, as now, was characteristic of both the majority and the minority. But there was a significant resolution of ideas and feelings so that the final word was a commitment to an open society, a proud affirmation in favor of an open marketplace for ideas and beliefs, and a healthy suspicion of the growth of arbitrary power whether in a religious or a secular society. The judgment of most of these men was adversely affected by some erroneous or partisan versions of historical events and by certain moral and theological abstractions. But when the abstractions acquired flesh as at the building site in Cincinnati, the Methodist editor denounced discrimination against workmen based on their being Irish and Catholic. Most editors eventually saw only evil in denying to the distressed of the world the assumed physical, political, and spiritual advantages of America or in imposing artificial limits on their upward mobility.

The most archaic of the editors' views from the modern perspective of permissiveness was the prohibitionist mentality applied to personal vices and public amusements. Joys that did not arise rather directly from piety were usually taboo, and this taboo included many artistic and cultural activities. These churchmen seemed even more convinced than the original Puritan of the power of their religion to decontaminate the individual and society with respect to the physical and moral ravages associated with such articles as alcohol and tobacco. Although modern science has underscored the validity of their concern, modern experience has underscored once more the victory of human nature in behalf of the vices. However archaic the prohibitory mentality may now appear, the same intellect and religious experience nourished concern to reduce the level of violence, also a venture in which they were less than totally successful. Sensitive men even caught the moral dilemma created by the conjunction of affluence and pride in the changing formalities associated with death as the frontier gave way to urban development. Men who might be dismissed patronizingly as moral bigots, nevertheless, gave the strongest possible endorsement to education and for the standard civic, moral, and economic reasons which went far beyond the minimal needs of reading for spiritual improvement. The only persons in the Old Northwest who could have given more enthusiastic support to education were professional educators themselves.

Evangelical editors of the era cultivated the characteristically American fondness for the oppressed with its powerful overtones of guilt. Some of them sought to disturb the conscience of Americans for the cruelties of the government's Indian policies. They publicized and urged support for all state and private agencies involved with the physically and mentally handicapped. On the other hand, they were less liberal than many of their contemporaries with regard to the criminal. They believed that retribution was legitimate in principle, they believed in personal accountability for acts of wrongdoing, and they believed in the priority of the rights of the law-abiding over the rights of the evil doer. It was the oppressed slave upon whom they lavished the most attention, if not deep affection. They presented exhaustively and with much repetition to their scores of thousands of readers the moral case against that institution. It is inconceivable that this carried no influence in contributing to the majority in the Old Northwest who eventually supported restrictive political action. They must also have furnished at least some of the motive force which would help sustain the ultimate victors through the "ordeal of union."

These editors contributed, and probably in no small way, to making moral outrage a national institution. Editors approached subjects such as slavery in largely religious, moralistic, and romantic terms. They founded papers with a dual function in order to apply just such values to secular society. The verbal picture of the fleeing slave or the imprisoned fugitive was the essence of slavery just as the picture of the shrunken body of a child nursing at the breast of its starving mother becomes the journalistic essence of a wide range of complex moral, social, political, and economic problems for modern man. The editors evoked guilt for both the nonrecognition of these objects of moral sentiment and for inaction once the religious press had done its duty toward making readers aware. To read of the plight of the slave and not to act made a person guilty just as sitting down to an abundant meal in contemporary America is an outrage against the starving. The theological abstractions proclaimed by these men may now seem archaic to many, but the facile identification of saints and sinners, the gauging of a system's failure by visionary expectations rather than reality, and assuming the perfectability of both means and goals are all represented to some degree in contemporary approaches to poverty, pollution, health, world peace, and racial justice—do these characteristics derive somewhat from those whose works this book examines?

Whatever the cause and effect relation may be, certainly the moralistic fevers which are endemic among Americans are fully compatible with the spirit of those who urged the evangelical regiments into combat with evil in the Old Northwest. In spite of theologies which made much of sin and evil they believed that their challenging environment was subject to reshaping by aggressive believers. Religious faith and activity were, in addition to their provisions for otherworldly guarantees, vehicles for cleansing secular institutions and sanctifying them to man's well-being. And although the triumph of righteousness was not automatic, these evangelicals were optimistic. They believed with President Abraham Lincoln that even the monumental tragedy of the Civil War, however it was bred and whosesoever guilt it was, would be morally productive. It seems that confidence of this sort may have faded in this society. Could it be in part the ironic result of the generations of guilt-inducing self-criticism centered in the lofty expectation that the world of human interests can finally be purged of selfishness and conflict? Now, of course, the professed instruments of salvation are not so much God, the religious experience, or religious newspapers, but rather courts, committees, computers, bureaucrats, and yet another corps of advocacy journalists.

NOTES
Chapter I

[1] Frank Luther Mott, *American Journalism: A History of Newspapers in the United States through 260 Years, 1690 to 1950*, revised edition (New York, 1950), 202-203.

[2] *Religious Telescope* (Circleville, Ohio), November 27, 1839.

[3] A. L. McKinney, *Life and Labors of I. N. Walter: Memoir of Elder Isaac N. Walter* (Cincinnati, 1857), 280.

[4] Albert Elijah Dunning, *Congregationalists in America* (New York, 1894), 477.

[5] *Presbyterian of the West* (Cincinnati), December 30, 1858.

[6] *Northwestern Christian Advocate* (Chicago), November 28, 1860.

[7] *Western Christian Advocate* (Cincinnati), January 29, 1851.

[8] *Northwestern Advocate*, August 24, 1853.

[9] Eugene P. Willging and Herta Hatzfeld, *Catholic Serials of the Nineteenth Century in the United States: A Descriptive Bibliography and Union List*, Second Series: Part Seven, Michigan (Washington, D.C., 1964), 24-27.

[10] W. W. McKinney, ed., *The Presbyterian Valley* (Pittsburgh, 1958), 300-304. *Weekly Recorder* (Chillicothe), July 5, 1814.

[11] Mott, *American Journalism*, 168-169; 200-206.

[12] James K. Lytle, *Twentieth Century History of Delaware County, Ohio and Representative Citizens* (Chicago, 1908), 188, 239. An ecumenical tone was also true of this agency in the South Atlantic States during this period. Henry Smith Stroupe, *The Religious Press in the South Atlantic States, 1802-1865; An Annotated Bibliography with Historical Introduction and Notes*. (Durham, N. C., 1956), 10-11.

[13] Mott, *American Journalism*, 204.

[14] Carlyle Buley, *The Old Northwest: Pioneer Period, 1815-1840*, II (Bloomington, Indiana, 1951), 46-50; 107.

[15] Frank J. Heinl, "Newspapers and Periodicals in the Lincoln-Douglas Country, 1831-1832," *Journal of the Illinois Historical Society*, XXIII (October, 1930), 411-420. Coming through the Jacksonville post office in 1831 were 243 religious newspapers. Of those identified, 87 came from outside the region and 22 from the area.

[16] Mott, *American Journalism*, 298-302.

[17] Millard G. Roberts, "The Methodist Book Concern in the West, 1800-1850," unpublished thesis (University of Chicago, 1942), 225-226. Mott, *American Journalism*, 303.

[18] Circulation figures are not uniformly available so estimates incorporate conservative judgments based upon known factors relative to the minimum patronage for survival.

[19] Edwin Scott Gaustad, *Historical Atlas of Religion in America*

(New York, 1962), 62;130. This source has maps showing the geographical distribution of the denominations by number of congregations. According to Assembly Minutes the Old School had in excess of 20,000 members in the Northwest in 1850; the New School, in excess of 30,000.

[20] *Observer and Telegraph* (Hudson), February 28, 1833.

[21] *Christian Herald* (Cincinnati), January 3, 1861.

[22] Joseph Camp Griffith Kennedy, "Catalogue of the Newspapers and Periodicals Published in the United States,.... Compiled from the United States Census Statistics of 1850." *Livingston's Law Register for 1852* (New York, 1852), 36.

[23] *Christian Herald,* January 3, 1861.

[24] Editorial quoted in *Presbyterian of the West,* June 28, 1855. *Central Christian Herald* (Cincinnati), July 12, 1855; January 29, 1857. *Presbyterian of the West,* February 7, 1850.

[25] *Northwestern Advocate,* February 21, 1855.

[26] Robert Samuel Fletcher, *A History of Oberlin College From its Foundations Through the Civil War,* I (Oberlin, 1943), 418-421. *Oberlin Evangelist,* March 13, 1839.

[27] Elmo Arnold Robinson, *The Universalist Church in Ohio* (Cincinnati, 1923), 139.

[28] *Star in the West* (Cincinnati), January 1, 1835; July 1, 1852.

[29] Rufus Babcock, *Forty Years of Pioneer Life: Memoirs of John Mason Peck* (Philadelphia, 1864), 234-239. *Western Pioneer* (Alton), June 29, August 10, 1838.

[30] *Christian Times* (Chicago), January 27, 1858. Baptist records show their population in the Northwest in excess of 65,000 by 1850.

[31] Kennedy, "Catalogue of Newspapers," 36. *Cross and Baptist Journal of the Mississippi Valley* (Cincinnati), August 26, 1836.

[32] Justin A. Smith, *A History of the Baptists in the Western States East of the Mississippi* (Philadelphia, 1896), 375-377.

[33] The General Conference in 1836 recommended that all unofficial papers be discontinued and no more commenced. In 1840 it gave specific instructions to itinerants in handling subscriptions. *Western Advocate,* June 3, 1836; July 10, 1840. Roberts, "Methodist Book Concern," 164-171. Methodist records show the membership in the Northwest at about 215,000 in 1850.

[34] Charles Cist, *Cincinnati in 1841: Its Early Annals and Future Prospects* (Cincinnati, 1841), 261-263. In 1929 Methodist papers became *The Christian Advocate, Western Edition* and *Northwestern Edition. Western Advocate,* October 9, 1835.

[35] *Methodist Correspondent* (Zanesville), November 14, 1835. Ancel H. Bassett, *A Concise History of the Methodist Protestant Church ...* (Pittsburgh, 1877), xxiii-xxiv; 176-185; 437-443. *Western Methodist Protestant* (Springfield), April 9, 1856.

[36] *Manual of the United Brethren Publishing House; Historical and Descriptive* (Dayton, 1832), 4, 17, 121-124. Henry G. Spayth and William Hanby, *History of the Church of the United Brethren in Christ* (Circleville, Ohio, 1851), 183-185; 236-239. *Religious Telescope,* December 13, 1834; June 29, 1853.

[37] Raymond W. Albright, *A History of the Evangelical Church* (Harrisburg, Pennsylvania, 1945), 187, 203-206. *Evangelical Messenger* (Cleveland), March 8, 1860.

[38] Willging and Hatzfeld, *Catholic Serials,* Part Twelve, Kentucky and Ohio (1966), 82-91.

[39] *Catholic Telegraph* (Cincinnati), August 17, 1837. Kennedy, "Catalogue of Newspapers," 36.

[40] *Catholic Telegraph,* January 3, 1852.

[41] *Western Episcopal Observer* (Gambier), October 9, 1841. *Western Episcopalian and Gambier Observer,* June 20, 1855.

[42] *Oberlin Evangelist,* December 22, 1858.

[43] C. V. Sheatsley, *History of the Evangelical Lutheran Joint Synod of Ohio and Other States from the Earliest Beginnings to 1919* (Columbus, 1919), 120-127. *Lutheran Standard* (New Philadelphia, Columbus), February 1, 1843; July 25, 1856. For information on the *Western Missionary* see issue of August 27, 1857 and for the *Evangelist,* the *Missionary* for November 17, 1857 and June 30, 1859.

[44] Henry K. Shaw, *Buckeye Disciples: A History of the Disciples of Christ in Ohio* (St. Louis, 1952), 114. Joseph Franklin and J. A. Headington, *The Life and Times of Benjamin Franklin* (St. Louis, 1879), 76-79, contains the most thorough discussion of contemporary Disciple's publishing activities. Claude E. Spencer, *Periodicals of the Disciples of Christ and Related Groups* (Canton, Missouri, 1943), 171. *American Christian Review* (Cincinnati), December 7, 1858. Some sources offer an estimate of 60,000 Disciples in Ohio and Indiana by 1850.

[45] *Israelite* (Cincinnati), June 29, 1855. Max B. May, *Isaac M. Wise, the Founder of American Judaism: A Biography* (New York, 1916), 252-254. Wise's own account of both papers is dealt with in Isaac M. Wise, *Reminiscences Translated from the German and Edited With an Introduction by David Philipson* (Cincinnati, 1901), 265-274; 292-294.

[46] *Kirke Tidende* (Milwaukee), February 1, 1860.

[47] Albert O. Barton, "The Beginnings of the Norwegian Press in America," *Wisconsin Historical Society Proceedings* (1916), 210-211.

[48] J. Magnus Rohne, *Norwegian American Lutheranism up to 1872* (New York, 1926), 139-140. Barton, *Beginnings,* 207.

[49] Oscar Fritiof Ander, *The Career and Influence of T. N. Hasselquist, a Swedish-American Clergyman, Journalist and Educator* (Rock

Island, 1931), 29, 239-240. Gothard Everett Arden, *Augustana Heritage: A History of the Augustana Lutheran Church* (Rock Island, 1963), 111-112.

[50] Willging and Hatzfeld, *Catholic Serials, Kentucky and Ohio*, 109-114.

[51] Willging and Hatzfeld, *Catholic Serials*, Part Three, Illinois (1961), 66-69. *Ibid.*, Part Two, Wisconsin (1960), 79-84; 91-92.

[52] Willging and Hatzfeld, *Catholic Serials*, Michigan, 16. *Ibid.*, Illinois, 115-116.

[53] *Manual of the Publishing House*, 121-124.

[54] Carl Wittke, *William Nast: Patriarch of German Methodism* (Detroit, 1959), 85.

[55] N. M. Liljegren, N. O. Westergeen, C. G. Wallenius, *Svenska Metodismen I Amerika* (Chicago, 1895), 539-540.

[56] Adolf Olson, *A Centenary History, as Related to the Baptist General Conference of America* [Scandinavian] (Chicago, 1952), 169.

[57] Cist, *Cincinnati*, 263.

[58] *Weekly Recorder*, December 13, 1820; March 12, 1821. *Western Intelligencer* (Cleveland), September 14, 1827. *Philanthropist* (Mt. Pleasant), September 18, 1845.

[59] *Religious Telescope*, November 25, 1846. *Western Christian* (Chicago), September 18, 1845. *Kirke Tidende*, December 30, 1851.

[60] *Ohio Observer* (Cleveland), October 30, 1839. *Lutheran Standard*, March 1, 1848.

[61] *Ohio Observer*, March 1, 1832; October 6, 1843. *Christian Times*, September 26, 1860. *Religious Telescope*, December 22, 1858.

[62] *Western Christian*, December 24, 1845

[63] *Catholic Telegraph*, August 21, 1841.

[64] *Christian Messenger* (Madison), May 15, 1846; August 7, 1845. *Star in the West*, October 25, 1834.

[65] *Cross and Journal*, December 22, 1843.

[66] *Christian Times*, November 19, 1856.

[67] *American Christian Review*, October 25, 1859.

[68] *Religious Telescope*, September 9, 1857; February 4, 1852. *Central Christian Herald*, May 25, 1854; November 12, 1857.

[69] Mott, *American Journalism*, 300.

[70] *Michigan Christian Herald*, March 6, 1843. *Gambier Observer*, June 23, 1852. *Religious Telescope*, November 12, 1847.

[71] Mott, *American Journalism*, 298.

[72] *Cincinnati Journal*, March 1, 1838.

[73] Wittke, *Nast*, 87.

[74] *Religious Telescope*, October 29, 1849; February 27, 1850; September 4, 1850; September 14, 1853.

[75] *Northwestern Advocate*, March 22, 1854; August 18, 1858.

[76] *Michigan Christian Herald,* January 4, 1847.
[77] *Western Advocate,* April 11, 1860. *Watchman of the Valley* (Cincinnati), March 2, 1843. *Religious Telescope,* February 7, 1849.
[78] *Presbyterian of the West,* March 18, 1855. *Central Christian Herald,* March 8, 1855.
[79] *Presbyterian of the West,* July 1, 1858.
[80] *Christian Register* (Zanesville), November 28, 1850.
[81] *Western Missionary,* September 14, 1854. *Central Christian Herald,* March 17, 1848.
[82] *Western Advocate,* February 27, 1861.
[83] *Religious Telescope,* October 1, 1851. *Prairie Herald,* (Chicago), May 20, 1851. *Ohio Observer,* September 10, 1851.

Chapter II

[1] *Cross and Journal,* August 1, 1845. The leading sources of biographical information in these several pages are denominational histories and encyclopedias. Albright, *A History of the Evangelical Church.* Bassett, *History of the Methodist Protestant Church.* William Cathcart, *The Baptist Encyclopaedia* . . . (Philadelphia, 1881). T. H. Colhouer, *Sketches of the Founders of the Methodist Protestant Church* (Pittsburgh, 1880). Eddy, *Universalism.* William M. Glasgow, *Cyclopedic Manual of the United Presbyterian Church in North America* . . . (Pittsburgh, 1903). Henry Eyster Jacobs and John A. W. Hass, eds. *The Lutheran Cyclopedia* (New York, 1899). Julius Bodensieck, *The Encyclopedia of the Lutheran Church* (Minneapolis, 1965). John Lawrence, *The History of the Church of the United Brethren in Christ in Two Volumes* (Dayton, 1868). Alfred Nevin, *Encyclopaedia of the Presbyterian Church in the United States of America, Including the Northern and Southern Assemblies* (Philadelphia, 1884). Matthew Simpson, *Cyclopaedia of Methodism* . . . (Philadelphia, 1878). Tiers, *Christian Portrait Gallery.* Willging and Hatzfeld, *Catholic Serials of the Nineteenth Century.*
[2] *Catholic Telegraph,* July 18, 1839.
[3] McKinney, *Walter,* 25.
[4] Franklin and Headington, *Life of Franklin,* 25.
[5] Bassett, *History of the Methodist Protestant Church,* 410, xxv.
[6] *Central Christian Herald,* June 24, 1858.
[7] *Western Star* (Jacksonville, Ill.), December 17, 1846.
[8] *Christian Age* (Cincinnati), December 27, 1855.
[9] Babcock, *Memoir, John Mason Peck,* 272.
[10] *Western Recorder* (Zanesville), November 2, 1843.
[11] *Observer and Telegraph,* May 2, 1831.
[12] *Western Recorder,* January 29, 1846.

[13] *Miscellaneous Repository* (Mt. Pleasant), November 15, 1830.
[14] *Northwestern Advocate*, July 19, 1854.
[15] *Kirke Tidende*, August 19, 1853.
[16] *Western Catholic Register* (Detroit), April 1, 1843.
[17] *Western Advocate*, November 12, 1851.
[18] *Central Christian Herald*, September 2, 1852.
[19] *Western Observer* (Jacksonville), May 22, 1830.
[20] *Miscellaneous Repository*, October 24, 1829. *Catholic Telegraph*, September 3, 1843.
[21] *Northwestern Advocate*, January 19, 1853.
[22] *Western Advocate*, July 26, 1848.
[23] *Christian Herald*, January 3, 1861.
[24] *Ohio Observer*, December 7, 1853.
[25] *Northwestern Advocate*, January 19, 1853.
[26] *Evangelical Messenger*, January 4, 1854.
[27] Albright, *History of the Evangelical Church*, 204.
[28] *Weekly Recorder*, November 20, 1818.
[29] *Western Advocate*, February 13, 1856.
[30] *Michigan Christian Herald*, June 20, 1853. *Presbyterian of the West*, June 11, 1855. *Religious Telescope*, July 15, 1835. *Evangelical Messenger*, January 21, 1858. *Western Advocate*, January 2, 1850.
[31] *Evangelical Messenger*, February 1, 1854.
[32] *Religious Telescope*, December 15, 1852.
[33] *Methodist Correspondent*, June 20, 1835.
[34] *Western Advocate*, March 9, October 12, 1853.
[35] *Religious Telescope*, January 17, 1849.
[36] *Northwestern Advocate*, July 29, 1857; June 23, 1858. Laurence W. Norton, "Social and Religous Issues as Reflected in the Poetry in Selected Religious Newspapers 1845-1857," unpublished research paper (Lamar University, 1966).
[37] Albright, *History of the Evangelical Church*, 204.
[38] *Religious Telescope*, June 29, 1853; April 23, 1845.
[39] *Ohio Observer*, April 12, 1854.
[40] *Presbyterian of the West*, September 22, 1841.
[41] *Cincinnati Journal*, March 8, 1833.
[42] *Western Christian*, January 14, 1846.
[43] *Religious Telescope*, July 11, 1849.
[44] *Christian Messenger*, October 25, 1843.
[45] *Gambier Observer*, May 28, 1830.
[46] *Religious Telescope*, May 15, 1861.
[47] *Methodist Correspondent*, June 20, 1835.
[48] *Christian Herald*, January 10, 1861.
[49] *Cincinnati Journal*, August 16, 1838.
[50] *Western Advocate*, August 1, 1834.

[51] *Central Christian Herald,* July 21, 1859.
[52] *Religious Telescope,* May 7, 1845.
[53] *Central Christian Herald,* December 14, 1854.
[54] *Religious Telescope,* June 23, 1847.
[55] *Western Advocate,* July 17, 1835; June 10, 1836.
[56] *Evangelical Messenger,* April 1, 1857.
[57] *Watchman of the Valley,* March 4, 1841.
[58] *Northwestern Advocate,* March 30, 1853.
[59] *Western Missionary,* March 1, 1855.
[60] *Watchman of the Valley,* September 2, 1841.
[61] *Christian Times,* August 27, 1856.
[62] *Western Advocate,* April 12, 1854.
[63] *Religious Telescope,* April 3, May 15, 1839.
[64] *Western Advocate,* June 11, 1856. The vote was Calvin Kingsley, 116; Elliott, 73; scattered, 22.
[65] *Religious Telescope,* July 29, 1846.

Chapter III

[1] William Warren Sweet, *The Story of Religion in America,* second revised edition (New York, 1950), 389. *Western Advocate,* March 27, 1840.
[2] *Ibid.,* September 26, 1834; June 7, 1839; January 24, 1840. *Cross and Journal,* April 15, 1836. *Ohio Observer,* July 16, 1840. *Religious Telescope,* February 18, April 1, 1846, *Christian Journal and Religious Intelligencer* (Cincinnati), May 25, September 17, 1830.
[3] *Olive Branch* (Chicago), December 28, 1853.
[4] *Journal and Intelligencer,* September 17, 1830.
[5] *Western Advocate,* March 4, 1857.
[6] *Western Recorder,* May 4, 1848.
[7] *Northwestern Advocate,* February 27, 1861.
[8] Ray Allen Billington, *The Protestant Crusade, 1800-1860: A Study of the Origins of American Nativism* (New York, 1938), 1-31; 129-130; 139-140.
[9] Sweet, *Story of Religion,* 222.
[10] Alfred G. Stritch, "Political Nativism in Cincinnati, 1830-1860," *American Catholic Historical Society Records,* XLVIII (September, 1937), 229-230.
[11] *Sweet, Story of Religion,* 271.
[12] *Western Intelligencer,* December 20, 1828. *Cincinnati Journal,* November 10, 1829.
[13] Willging and Hatzfeld, *Catholic Serials,* Kentucky and Ohio, 83.

[14] *Catholic Telegraph,* November 26, 1831.
[15] *Ibid.,* December 6, 1833; January 28, November 3, 1832.
[16] *Ibid.,* April 25, 1834.
[17] *Gambier Observer,* February 20, 1835.
[18] Billington, *Protestant Crusade,* 68-76.
[19] *Standard* (Cincinnati), September 5, November 14, 1834.
[20] *Cincinnati Journal,* September 12, 1834.
[21] *Catholic Telegraph,* August 29, 1834.
[22] Billington, *Protestant Crusade,* 99-108.
[23] *Western Advocate,* September 2, 1836.
[24] *Religious Telescope,* March 8, 1837. *Western Advocate,* September 2, 1836.
[25] *Catholic Telegraph,* June 16, August 25, 1836.
[26] Billington, *Protestant Crusade,* 301. *Western Advocate,* November 9, 1853. *Religious Telescope,* January 18, 1854.
[27] Billington, *Protestant Crusade,* 308.
[28] *Presbyterian of the West,* October 28, 1852. *Religious Telescope,* November 21, 1849. *Christian Register,* May 16, 1850.
[29] These were all ecumenical efforts in Cincinnati and included the *True Catholic* (1844), the *Western Protestant* (1845), the *Anti-Papist* (1846-1847), and the *Cincinnati Protestant* (1847.)
[30] Stritch, "Nativism in Cincinnati," 259-263.
[31] Quoted *verbatim* in *Presbyterian of the West,* March 3, 1853 and *Western Advocate,* March 2, 1853.
[32] *Catholic Telegraph,* June 8, June 22, December 14, 1850; December 11, 1852; March 5, 1853.
[33] *Watchman of the Prairies,* (Chicago), September 18, 1849. *Ohio Observer,* August 1, 1849.
[34] *Western Advocate,* March 30, 1853. *Star in the West,* April 16, 1853.
[35] *Catholic Telegraph,* April 9, 1853.
[36] *Western Advocate,* February 4, 1842. *Northwestern Baptist* (Chicago), September 20, 1844. *Oberlin Evangelist,* March 1, 1848.
[37] *Watchman of the Praries,* September 16, 1851.
[38] *Christian Times,* June 22, 1854.
[39] *Watchman of the Valley,* March 16, 1843. *Central Christian Herald,* October 31, 1850. *Watchman of the Prairies,* September 14, 1852. *Michigan Christian Herald,* September 9, 1852.
[40] Billington, *Protestant Crusade,* 394-396. One might question Billington's conclusion that the greater success of Know Nothings in the Northeast was due primarily to the greater effectiveness of anti-Catholic propaganda. If western editors were less effective it was not because of a lapse of time or a lack of animosity or of skill. It would seem more likely that their concern was diluted by conditions peculiar

to the West and chiefly by the competition of the Republican party. Joseph Schafer, "Know-Nothingism in Wisconsin," *Wisconsin Magazine of History,* VIII (September, 1924), 3-21. John P. Senning, "The Know-Nothing Movement in Illinois, 1854-1856," *Illinois Historical Society Journal,* VIII (April, 1914), 7-33. Eugene H. Roseboom, "Salmon P. Chase and the Know Nothings," *Mississippi Valley Historical Review,* XXV (December, 1938), 335-350.

[41] *Western Advocate,* May 17, June 28, October 25, 1854.

[42] *Ibid.,* August 30, 1854.

[43] *Northwestern Advocate,* September 20, 1854; January 19, 1855.

[44] *Religious Telescope,* November 16, 23, 1853; May 21, August 10, December 20, 1854; February 14, October 17, 1855. *Christliche Botschafter* (Cleveland), June 14, 1854. *Christliche Apologete* (Cincinnati), June 19, 1854. *Oberlin Evangelist,* August 2, 1854; Janaury 3, 1855. *Michigan Christian Herald,* September 1, October 26, 1854; June 21, 1855. *Free Presbyterian* (Yellow Springs), December 20, 1854.

[45] *Kirke Tidende,* February 23, 1852. Ander, *Hasselquist,* 32-33; 41, 154.

[46] *Catholic Telegraph,* August 26, April 1, June 25, March 18, 25, 1854; April 14, 1855.

[47] *Ibid.,* October 21, 1854.

[48] Rufus Learsi, *The Jews in America: A History* (Cleveland and New York, 1954), 68-73; 76-78.

[49] *Western Advocate,* September 21, 1853. *Western Missionary,* April 13, 1854.

[50] *Israelite* (Cincinnati), September 22, 1854.

[51] *Religious Telescope,* December 5, 1849; February 6, 1850; August 11, 1854.

[52] *Israelite,* August 11, 1854.

[53] *Ibid.,* July 20, October 3, 1855.

[54] *Ibid.,* June 19, 1857; December 22, 1854.

[55] *Weekly Recorder,* March 19, 1819.

[56] *Religious Telescope,* October 17, 1838.

[57] *Northwestern Baptist,* April 18, 1843.

[58] Quoted from the *Northwestern Baptist* in *Better Covenant* (Rockford), February 2, 1843.

[59] *Star in the West,* June 25, 1853; December 12, 1835; December 17, 1842; April 19, 1845.

[60] *Ibid.,* June 5, August 28; 1830; January 7, February 4, 1832; June 27; 1840. *Better Covenant,* February 2, 1843.

[61] *Star in the West,* September 26, 1840; January 28, 1841.

[62] Alice Felt Tyler, *Freedom's Ferment: Phases of American Social History from the Colonial Period to the Outbreak of the Civil War,* Harper Torchbook edition (New York, 1962), 86-107.

[63] *Cincinnati Journal*, December 28, 1832. *Gambier Observer*, August 30, 1833. *Religious Telescope*, December 12, 1838. *Star in the West*, February 20, 1841.

[64] *Gambier Observer*, August 30, 1833.

[65] *Religious Telescope*, December 12, 1838.

[66] *Star in the West*, July 20, 1844. *Western Recorder*, July 18, 1844. *Presbyterian of the West*, July 18, 1844. *Religious Telescope*, July 31, 1844. *Baptist Helmet* (Vandalia), September 24, 1846. *Cross and Journal*, September 25, 1846.

[67] *Catholic Telegraph*, November 28, 1857. *Kirke Tidende*, February 25, 1858.

[68] *Western Advocate*, April 11, 1860.

[69] *Cross and Journal*, April 10, 1840; May 12, 1843.

[70] *Christian Messenger*, October 31, 1844. *Western Advocate*, March 31, 1843. *Presbyterian of the West*, April 20, May 4, 1843.

[71] *Glad Tidings and Ladies Universalist* (Akron), February 12, 1840. *Star in the West*, April 29, 1843; October 26, 1844. *Catholic Telegraph*, September 23, 1844.

[72] *Western Midnight Cry* (Cincinnati), January 20, 1844.

[73] *Ibid.*, March 2, 1844.

[74] The origins and scope of Spiritualism are described in Earl Wesley Fornell, *The Unhappy Medium: Spiritualism and the Life of Margaret Fox* (Austin, Texas, 1964). Tyler, *Freedom's Ferment*, 82-85.

[75] *Ohio Observer*, April 21, 1851; November 24, 1852.

[76] *Gospel Herald* (Madison, Indiana), April 21, 1855.

[77] *Israelite*, October 14, 1859.

Chapter IV

[1] Foster Rhea Dulles, *A History of Recreation: America Learns to Play*, second edition (New York, 1965), 84-88.

[2] The role of revivalism and perfectionism in social reform has been rather thoroughly canvassed in Charles C. Cole, Jr., *The Social Ideas of the Northern Evangelists, 1826-1860* (New York, 1954), and Timothy L. Smith, *Revivalism and Social Reform: American Protestantism on the Eve of the Civil War* (Nashville, 1955), as well as in earlier works dealing with specific issues such as Gilbert Hobbes Barnes, *The Antislavery Impulse, 1830-1844* (New York, 1933). The former two use relatively few sources from west of New York, however, and this is especially true of religious newspapers. Barnes used few of the religious newspapers available.

[3] *Methodist Correspondent*, December 20, 1834.

[4] *Evangelical Messenger*, May 2, 1855.

[5] *Oberlin Evangelist*, July 30, 1851; January 5, 1853.

[6] *Alton Observer*, September 8, 1836; January 26, 1837.

[7] *Ohio Observer*, June 16, 30, 1836.

[8] *Cincinnati Journal*, August 12, 19, 1831.

[9] *Religious Telescope*, December 3, 1845. *Presbyterian of the West*, April 23, 1857.

[10] *Western Advocate*, September 29, 1852. *Catholic Telegraph*, January 9, 1858.

[11] *Israelite*, June 29, 1860.

[12] *Catholic Telegraph*, July 24, 1858. *Star in the West*, May 16, 1840; November 8, 1856.

[13] *Western Episcopal Observer* (Gambier), February 12, 1851. *Indiana Religious Intelligencer* (Indianapolis), August 22, 1828. *Lutheran Standard*, April 25, 1849.

[14] *Evangelical Messenger*, March 7, 1861. *Northwestern Advocate*, March 13, 1861.

[15] Dulles, *History of Recreation*, 131-137.

[16] *Weekly Recorder*, July 2, 1819.

[17] *Ohio Observer*, July 16, 1835. *Northwestern Baptist*, August 15, 1844. *Michigan Christian Herald*, October 11, 1847.

[18] *Western Recorder*, May 1, 1851.

[19] *Western Tablet* (Chicago), September 10, 1853.

[20] *Presbyterian of the West*, March 13, 1856. *Star in the West*, March 29, 1856.

[21] *Western Advocate*, February 11, June 23, 1852; April 3, June 29, 1859.

[22] *Western Recorder*, August 26, 1840.

[23] *Watchman of the Valley*, October 14, 1847.

[24] *Israelite*, November 12, 1858.

[25] *Catholic Telegraph*, April 28, 1836.

[26] Dulles, *History of Recreation*, 100-121.

[27] *Presbyterian of the West*, July 8, 1857.

[28] *Witness* (Indianapolis), October 20, 1858. *Catholic Telegraph*, April 2, 1846.

[29] *Congregational Herald*, April 28, 1854. Dulles, *History of Recreation*, 114.

[30] Carl Bode, *The Anatomy of American Popular Culture, 1840-1861* (Berkeley, 1959), 35-36.

[31] *Central Christian Herald*, April 17, 24, 1851. *Western Advocate*, April 23, 1851.

[32] *Oberlin Evangelist*, September 29, 1852.

[33] *Lutheran Standard*, November 17, 1854. *Presbyterian of the West*, November 9, 1854.

[34] *Gambier Observer*, October 17, 1834. *Ohio Observer*, June 6, 1844. *Star in the West*, September 16, 1843.

[35] *Catholic Telegraph,* December 10, 1846.

[36] *Michigan Christian Herald,* August 26, 1858. *United Presbyterian of the West* (Monmouth), August 4, 1858.

[37] *Northwestern Advocate,* February 24, 1858. *Western Advocate,* November 7, 1834; April 9, 1856.

[38] *Ibid.,* March 13, 1846; July 30, 1847.

[39] *Catholic Telegraph,* April 9, 1846.

[40] *Watchman of the Valley,* August 24, 1848.

[41] *Western Advocate,* July 3, 1835; June 23, 1837. *Star in the West,* July 19, 1856.

[42] *Western Advocate,* June 27, 1849.

[43] *Catholic Telegraph,* July 10, 1835.

[44] *Presbyterian of the West,* December 22, 1853.

[45] *Lutheran Standard,* November 10, 1843.

[46] *Evangelical Messenger,* June 7, 1854; November 22, 1859.

[47] *Weekly Recorder,* July 12, 19, 1814; July 26, 1815; June 22, 1820.

[48] *Gambier Observer,* January 21, 1831. *Presbyterian of the West,* March 1, 1855. *Oberlin Evangelist,* August 29, 1849.

[49] There is a concise summary of the Sabbatarian Movement in Cole, *Social Ideas of Northern Evangelists,* 106-109. *Western Intelligencer,* May 26, 1829. *Indiana Religious Intelligencer,* February 13, 1829. *Pandect,* January 13, March 3, 1829.

[50] *Star in the West,* April 24, January 16, 1830.

[51] *Catholic Telegraph,* December 11, 1845; May 11, May 24, 1849; September 3, 1859.

[52] *Cincinnati Journal,* November 12, 1830.

[53] *Presbyterian of the West,* May 29, 1856.

[54] *Gambier Observer,* June 28, 1837.

[55] *Western Universalist* (Terre Haute), April 19, 1845. *Religious Telescope,* July 18, 1849; June 25, 1851.

[56] *Philanthropist,* July 23, 1818. *Weekly Recorder,* October 30, 1816.

[57] Tyler, *Freedom's Ferment,* 325-326. Cole, *Social Ideas of Northern Evangelists,* 120-124. *Indiana Religious Intelligencer,* September 11, June 26, 1829.

[58] *Ohio Observer,* November 16, 1833. Tyler, *Freedom's Ferment,* 336. *Gambier Observer,* July 10, 1835; October 14, 1831; March 20, 1835.

[59] *Religious Telescope,* August 12, September 9, 1835. *Cross and Journal,* July 11, 1834.

[60] *Michigan Christian Herald,* December 8, 1853. *Kirke Tidende,* January 27, February 9, 1852.

[61] *Star in the West,* May 8, 1830; August 22, 1840; August 27, 1854.

[62] *Catholic Telegraph,* April 18, 1840; April 16, 1846; September 9, 23, 1847; March 20, 1852.

[63] Tyler, *Freedom's Ferment*, 346. *Western Recorder*, August 17, 1848. *Presbyterian of the West*, October 16, 1851. *Catholic Telegraph*, September 11, 1841.

[64] *Western Missionary*, August 31, 1852.

[65] Bode, *Anatomy of American Culture*, 96-99. *Watchman of the Valley*, November 16, 1848. *Presbyterian of the West*, November 22, 1848.

[66] *Western Advocate*, November 8, 28, 1848.

[67] *Catholic Telegraph*, November 23, 1848.

[68] *Oberlin Evangelist*, August 4, 1858; November 6, 1839.

[69] The extra was dated February 24, 1841.

[70] *Oberlin Evangelist*, December 20, 1843.

[71] Cole, *Social Ideas of Northern Evangelists*, 126-129. *Observer and Telegraph*, July 4, 1833.

[72] *Northwestern Advocate*, March 9, 1859.

[73] *Western Advocate*, May 4, 1859. *Congregational Herald*, March 15, 1859.

[74] *Western Advocate*, January 6, 1858.

[75] Richard Wires, "The Divorce Issue and Reform in Nineteenth Century Indiana," Ball State Monograph Number Eight, *Publications in History*, No. 2 (Muncie, Indiana, 1967).

[76] *Catholic Telegraph*, February 15, 1849. *Herald and Era*, February 16, 1856. *Ohio Observer*, March 14, 1849. *Northwestern Advocate*, June 10, 1857; June 15, 1859. *Presbyterian of the West*, June 17, 1858.

[77] *Western Advocate*, August 15, 1849. *Lutheran Standard*, August 29, 1849. *Central Christian Herald*, January 9, 1851. *Catholic Telegraph*, June 21, 1856.

[78] *Presbyterian of the West*, January 8, 1852. *Evangelical Messenger*, January 7, 1858.

[79] Witke, *Nast*, 107-108. *Western Advocate*, May 2, 1858.

[80] *Ohio Observer*, October 19, 1853.

[81] *Western Advocate*, May 20, 1836. *Prairie Herald*, January 13, 1852. *Ohio Observer*, October 19, 1853. *Oberlin Evangelist*, August 17, 1853.

[82] *Ohio Observer*, October 19, 1853. *Western Recorder*, July 21, 1853. *Oberlin Evangelist*, January 7, 1857.

[83] *Western Advocate*, September 28, 1853. *Gambier Observer*, February 22, 1833. *Lutheran Standard*, May 18, 1844.

[84] *Western Tablet*, October 1, 1853.

[85] *Star in the West*, October 27, 1855. *Western Advocate*, October 24, 1855. *Michigan Christian Herald*, February 21, 1856.

[86] *Cincinnati Journal*, May 25, 1830. *United Presbyterian of the West*, October 4, 1858. *Western Advocate*, September 1, 1858.

[87] *Western Recorder,* December 8, 1841.
[88] *Western Advocate,* January 13, 1837.
[89] *Philanthropist,* July 15, 1820. *Star in the West,* January 23, 1836.
[90] *Lutheran Standard,* December 21, 1842.
[91] *Western Episcopal Observer,* October 23, 1841; April 2, 1842.
[92] *Oberlin Evangelist,* April 14, 1832. *Western Advocate,* January 19, 1859. *Western Recorder,* July 31, 1845.
[93] *Michigan Christian Herald,* September 16, 1858.
[94] *Catholic Telegraph,* September 7, 1850; February 14, 1851.
[95] Dulles, *History of Recreation,* 144-146. *Michigan Christian Herald,* November 4, 1858. *Israelite,* May 4, 1860.
[96] *Baptist Weekly Journal,* September 6, 1833. *Catholic Telegraph,* December 27, 1851.
[97] *Ibid.,* February 10, 1848; October 31, 1857; July 31, 1858.
[98] *Lutheran Standard,* May 23, 1849.
[99] *Central Watchman,* June 22, 1849. *Presbyterian of the West,* September 18, 1851. *Presbyter,* November 10, 1859.

Chapter V

[1] *Cincinnati Journal,* November 23, 1832.
[2] *Observer and Telegraph,* August 18, 1829. Cole, *Northern Evangelists,* 140.
[3] *Cincinnati Journal,* January 4, 1838.
[4] *Weekly Recorder,* July 10, 1818; September 18, 1817. For some views on the relationship of the churches to the political and economic issues in the Jackson era see Cole, *Northern Evangelists,* 132-157; 165-191. T. Scott Miyakawa, *Protestants and Pioneers: Individualism and Conformity on the American Frontier* (Chicago, 1964), 55, 60, 199-206. Arthur Schlesinger, *The Age of Jackson* (Boston, 1950), 350-360. Russel B. Nye, *The Cultural Life of the New Nation* (New York, 1960), 220-221.
[5] *Western Intelligencer,* February 6, April 2, December 6, 1828.
[6] *Western Advocate,* October 3, 1834; July 31, 1840; January 6, 1843.
[7] *Cross and Journal,* November 6, 1840. *Gambier Observer,* March 29, 1838; October 7, 1831.
[8] *Western Advocate,* October 3, 1834.
[9] *Star in the West,* August 5, 1840.
[10] *Cincinnati Journal,* November 23, 1832. *Western Recorder,* October 7, 1840. *Gambier Observer,* March 20, 1841.
[11] *Oberlin Evangelist,* November 20, 1844. *Cincinnati Observer,* August 13, 1840. *Religious Telescope,* September 27, 1843.

[38] *Watchman of the Valley,* July 20, 1843.
[39] *Catholic Telegraph,* March 16, 1850.
[12] *Western Advocate,* January 6, 1843.
[13] *Western Recorder,* July 15, 1842; July 11, 1844. *Watchman of the Valley,* June 9, 1842.
[14] *Western Advocate,* August 11, 1843.
[15] *Methodist Correspondent,* September 26, 1835. *Western Recorder,* January 2, May 23, 1844.
[16] *Michigan Christian Herald,* October 24, 1850.
[17] *Watchman of the Valley,* October 20, 1842. *Primitive Expounder,* March 26, 1846. *Gospel Herald,* March 6, 1852.
[18] *Western Recorder,* May 2, 1844.
[19] *Western Advocate,* February 25, 1857. *Cross and Journal,* August 4, 1843. *Watchman of the Prairies,* March 20, 1849.
[20] *Catholic Telegraph,* February 2, 1850; November 13, 1852; April 1, 1854; September 6, 1851.
[21] *Western Midnight Cry,* March 16, May 18, 1844.
[22] *Religious Telescope,* April 2, 1856; August 12, September 9, 1857; July 18, 1860.
[23] *Western Missionary,* February 1, 1849; January 18, 1855.
[24] *Western Advocate,* November 30, December 14, 1853.
[25] *Western Tablet,* March 19, 1853. *Catholic Telegraph,* May 14, 1853; March 27, 1858.
[26] *Ohio Observer,* June 14, 1848.
[27] *Presbyterian of the West,* June 12, 1851.
[28] *Religious Telescope,* January 9, 1839; February 1, 1854; December 3, 1856.
[29] *Methodist Correspondent,* March 14, 1835. *Christian Messenger,* December 20, 1843. *Ohio Observer,* December 21, 1837.
[30] *Western Advocate,* July 8, October 14, November 11, 1857.
[31] *Israelite,* June 27, 1856.
[32] *Herald of the Prairies,* June 20, 1848. *Western Herald,* April 8, 1846. *Presbyterian of the West,* series of six September 6—October 18, 1849. *Church Record* (Chicago), September 1, 1859. *Evangelical Messenger,* August 8, 1855. *Michigan Christian Herald,* July 19, 1860.
[33] *Presbyterian of the West,* September 6, 1849.
[34] *Western Missionary,* July 21, 1853.
[35] *Western Pioneer,* October 23, 1837. *Western Advocate,* January 21, 1842. *Western Missionary,* April 1, 1851.
[36] *Western Advocate,* January 21, 1842. *Catholic Telegraph,* January 15, 1842.
[37] *Evangelical Messenger,* November 11, 1857. *United Presbyterian of the West,* October 8, 1857.

[40] *Religious Telescope,* April 3, 1851; April 21, 1858.

[41] *Cross and Baptist Journal,* October 30, 1835.

[42] *Religious Telescope,* May 6, 1857. *Western Advocate,* January 20, May 23, 1860.

[43] *Western Missionary,* August 31, 1854. *Presbyterian of the West,* December 13, 1855.

[44] *Journal and Messenger,* May 6, 1853; January 20, 1860.

[45] *Western Advocate,* June 8, 1853. *Lutheran Standard,* September 7, 1853.

[46] *Cross and Journal,* July 18, 1845.

[47] *Western Episcopalian,* March 23, 1853. *Western Advocate,* January 25, 1839.

[48] *Western Advocate,* March 30, 1838; May 6, 1842; June 29, December 14, 1838; February 4, 1842.

[49] *Ohio Observer,* October 1, 1851.

[50] *Western Advocate,* August 17, 1853.

[51] *Central Watchman,* August 24, 1849.

[52] *Israelite,* January 12, 1855; November 12, 1858.

[53] *Western Advocate,* April 21, 1852; November 1, 1854.

[54] *Catholic Telegraph,* July 6, 1837; June 5, 1858.

[55] For the ambivalent feelings of churchmen toward higher education and professional ministerial training 1830-1850 see Richard Hofstadter, *Anti-intellectualism in American Life,* First Vintage edition (New York, 1966), 95-106. Miyakawa, *Protestants and Pioneers,* 80-101. *Western Advocate,* January 2, 9, 1835. *Ohio Observer,* February 20, 1834. *Western Advocate,* December 21, 1842. *Presbyterian of the West,* January 19, 1843.

[56] Miyakawa, *Protestants and Pioneers,* 31, 99-101.

[57] *Israelite,* July 28, 1854.

[58] *Observer and Telegraph,* January 27, 1831; March 23, July 5, 1832.

[59] *Cincinnati Journal,* September 29, 1829; December 3, 1830.

[60] *Philanthropist,* June 9, 1821. *Indiana Religious Intelligencer,* January 16, 1829. *Cross and Journal,* December 1, 1837; February 16, 1838.

[61] *Ohio Observer,* September 1, 1842. *Oberlin Evangelist,* September 14, 1842.

[62] *Western Star,* May 20, June 11, 1845.

[63] *Watchman of the Valley,* May 7, 1846.

[64] *Prairie Herald,* March 16, 1852. *Western Advocate,* January 21, 1852. *Michigan Christian Herald,* January 1, 1852. *Western Missionary,* January 20, 1852.

[65] *Catholic Telegraph,* December 6, 1851; January 3, 1852.

[66] *Northwestern Advocate,* August 31, 1853; September 8, 1858. *Presbyterian of the West,* June 29, 1854.
[67] *Western Missionary,* September 15, 1854. *Michigan Christian Herald,* June 8, 1849. *Catholic Telegraph,* August 9, 1851. *Western Friend* (Cincinnati), January 11, 1849.
[68] *Religious Telescope,* April 23, 1845. *Western Observer,* September 25, 1830.
[69] *Western Recorder,* October 31, 1839. *Western Advocate,* November 17, 1843.
[70] *United Presbyterian of the West,* February 25, 1857. *Presbyterian of the West,* May 19, 1853. *Central Christian Herald,* April 7, 1853.
[71] *Central Watchman,* August 24, 1849.
[72] *Western Advocate,* July 1, 1857.

Chapter VI

[1] Gilbert Hobbes Barnes, *The Antislavery Impulse, 1830-1844* (New York, 1933).

[2] Dwight Lowell Dumond, *Antislavery Origins of the Civil War in the United States,* Ann Arbor paperback (1959), 98-114.

[3] *Weekly Recorder,* December 23, 1819; February 9, 1820. *Philanthropist,* October 17, 1817; August 23, 1820.

[4] *Oberlin Evangelist,* January 30, May 22, September 11, 1839.

[5] *Alton Observer,* February 2, June 22, January 26, August 17, 1837.

[6] *Western Pioneer,* March 29, April 28, 1837.

[7] *Ibid.,* January 18, February 1, 1838.

[8] William Warren Sweet, *Religion on the American Frontier: The Baptists* (New York, 1931), 97. Harry Thomas Stock, "Protestantism in Illinois before 1835," *Journal of the Illinois State Historical Society,* XII (April, 1919), 3. *Western Pioneer,* July 29, 1836.

[9] *Cross and Journal,* May 8, 1835; November 17, 1837.

[10] *Cincinnati Journal,* January 26, 1830; September 7, October 5, 1832; June 6, May 16, October 10, May 30, 1834; April 24, August 28, 1835.

[11] *Ohio Observer,* November 23, 1837. *Observer and Telegraph,* January 17, 1833. *Ohio Observer,* September 5, 1833; February 25, 1836; May 2, 1833.

[12] *Religious Telescope,* January 24, 1838; May 31, 1837; May 15, 1839; August 31, 1842. *Manual United Brethren Publishing House,* 116-117.

[13] Donald G. Mathews, *Slavery and Methodism: A Chapter in American Morality, 1780-1845* (Princeton, 1965), 113-176.

[14] *Western Advocate,* August 14, 1835; January 5, 1838.

[15] *Ibid.,* April 23, 1841.

[16] *Western Recorder,* November 11, 1842.

[17] *Gambier Observer,* July 5, October 18, 1833; April 25, 1834; May 29, 1835. *Star in the West,* October 12, 1833; December 17, 1842. Robinson, *Universalist Church in Ohio,* 122. *Catholic Telegraph,* December 31, 1835; March 14, 1840.

[18] L. Wesley Norton, "The Religious Press and the Compromise of 1850: A Study of the Relationship of the Methodist, Baptist, and Presbyterian Press to the Slavery Controversy 1846-1851," unpublished dissertation (University of Illinois, 1959). Clayton Sumner Ellsworth, "The American Churches and the Mexican War," *American Historical Review,* XLV (January, 1940), 301-326. This survey indicates a variety of opinions even though the preponderance of views expressed in Protestant papers in the Northwest left no doubt of their intense disapproval.

[19] *Oberlin Evangelist,* July 29, 1840; November 20, 1844; June 22, 1848.

[20] *Ibid.,* August 16, September 13, 1848; October 30, November 6, 1850; July 7, December 8, 1852.

[21] *Western Herald,* September 23, 1846; August 23, 1848; February 28, 1849.

[22] *Watchman of the Valley,* April 21, 1842; September 28, November 2, 1848.

[23] *Central Christian Herald,* January 10, March 21, April 4, October 3, November 7, 1850; January 16, 1851; March 25, 1852.

[24] *Western Advocate,* April 10, December 11, 1846; November 15, 1848; October 9, 1850.

[25] *Watchman of the Prairies,* October 19, November 2, 30, 1847; June 13, August 29, 1848; April 2, 1850.

[26] References contained in a series of editorials *Cross and Journal,* November 27, 1846—March 12, 1847.

[27] *Religious Telescope,* March 12, 1845; October 21, 1846; November 1, 1848; October 16, 1850; September 29, 1852.

[28] *Methodist Recorder,* October 24, 1844. Allbeck, *Lutherans in Ohio,* 172-175. *Lutheran Standard,* January 25, March 8, 1843; May 31, 1844. Charles W. Heathecote, *The Lutheran Church and the Civil War* (New York, 1919), 60-62. Don C. Markham, "The Civil War as it was Seen by Members of the Reformed Church in the United States," unpublished thesis (Theological Seminary of the Evangelical and Reformed Church, Lancaster, Pennsylvania, 1959). *Presbyterian of the West,* August 8, November 7, December 12, 1850.

[29] *Texas Christian Advocate* (Galveston), May 31, 1860.

[30] Edmund Lacey, "Reaction of Major Protestant Denominations to the Kansas-Nebraska Bill of 1854," unpublished thesis (Lamar State College, 1965).

[31] The names are given in the *Congressional Globe: Appendix,* Thirty-third Congress, First Session, 1854, XXIX (Washington, D.C., 1854), 654.

[32] Lacey, "Reaction to Kansas-Nebraska Bill," 81-82. *Letter of Senator Douglas, Vindicating His Character ... Against the Assaults Contained in the Proceedings of a Public Meeting Composed of Twenty-five Clergymen of Chicago* (Washington, 1854).

[33] *Congregational Herald,* February 17, March 3, April 28, May 5, June 2, 1854. *Northwestern Advocate* April 26, 1854. George Harmon, "The Northern Clergy and the Impending Crisis, 1850-1860," *Pennsylvania Magazine of History and Biography,* LXV (April, 1941) 171-201. Harmon reached the erroneous conclusion on the basis of a sampling of chiefly Old School Presbyterian and Lutheran spokesmen that Douglas received the support of the clergy more generally. The conclusion was reached without benefit of the religious newspapers.

[34] *Oberlin Evangelist,* March 12, July 2, November 19, 1856; September 12, November 21, 1860.

[35] *Congregational Herald,* April 16, May 7, 1857; October 14, 1858; October 11, November 15, 1860.

[36] *Central Christian Herald,* May 25, 1854; August 28, October 30, December 25, 1856. Issues are not available for the campaign in 1860.

[37] *Ohio Observer,* July 12, 26, 1848; February 1, 15, March 29, June 7, October 18, 1854. The *Observer* was sold to an eastern paper before further political developments.

[38] *Presbyterian of the West,* February 2, March 2, 23, 1854; September 12, 1855; February 14, 21, July 17, 24, 1856; July 5, September 27, October 18, 1860.

[39] *United Presbyterian of the West,* March 18, 1857; November 14, 1859; February 6, May 28, July 16, November 19, 1860.

[40] See the journals for the area conferences. For the Michigan and Detroit Annual Conferences see Wesley Norton, "The Methodist Episcopal Church in Michigan and the Politics of Slavery: 1850-1860," *Michigan History,* XLVIII (September, 1964), 193-213.

[41] *Western Advocate,* May 31, October 18, 1854; August 6, October 1, 8, 1856; February 10, April 14, 1858; October 31, 1860.

[42] *Northwestern Advocate,* February 8, July 26, October 18, 1854; July 16, October 29, 1856.

[43] *Ibid.,* September 8, 29, 1858; October 12, 1859; July 11, August 15, 22, September 26, 1860. For Cartwright's early activities see Stock, "Protestantism in Illinois," 10-11.

[44] *Christliche Apologete,* November 15, 1855; August 7, 1856; October 25, 1860. Witke, *Nast,* 110.

[45] *Cross and Journal,* February 1, November 14, 1856. *Christian Times,* June 4, November 5, 1856; May 23, June 27, 1860. *Michigan Christian Herald,* April 17, October 30, November 13, 1856; August 9, November 15, 1860.

[46] *Religious Telescope,* September 27, 1854; July 9, October 29, 1856; May 23, June 6, 13, 1860. *Froeliche Botschafter* (Dayton), October 2, 1856; May 24, July 5, 1860. *Christliche Botschafter,* December 3, 1859; July 7, November 10, 1860. *Evangelical Messenger,* July 12, 1860.

[47] Ander, *Hasselquist,* 113, 154-159. *Kirke Tidende,* July 2, October 9, 1852; August 29, 1854. Later issues were not available.

[48] *Lutheran Standard,* July 25, 1856; December 14, 1860. Markham, *Civil War and the Reformed Church,* 5-31. *Western Missionary,* July 12, 26, 1860. It may be significant that Buchanan was a member of this denomination and a member of the board of trustees of Mercer College, A Reformed institution.

[49] *Chicago Record,* December 15, 1860.

[50] *American Christian Review,* November 9, 1858; March 15, 1859; April 23, November 27, 1860.

[51] *Christian Luminary* (Cincinnati), June 2, September 8, October 20, 1859. The Disciples were generally moderate on the issue of slavery. David Edwin Harrell, *Quest for a Christian America...* (Nashville, 1966), 91-138.

[52] *Catholic Telegraph,* December 1, 1860; March 16, 1861. *Wahrheitsfreund* (Cincinnati), May 29, 1856.

[53] Learsi, *Jews in America,* 92-94.

[54] *Israelite,* November 30, 1860; January 4, February 1, 1861.

[55] *Ibid.,* February 8, April 19, 1861.

[56] *Western Missionary,* January 24, June 27, 1861. *Lutheran Standard,* April 26, June 7, 1861.

[57] *Star in the West,* June 8, September 28, November 16, 1861.

[58] *Chicago Record,* May 1, 1861; *Western Episcopalian,* April 25, 1861.

[59] *Catholic Telegraph,* April 20, May 18, 1861.

[60] V. Jacque Voegeli, *Free but not Equal: The Midwest and the Negro During the Civil War* (Chicago, 1967). Leon F. Litwack, *North of Slavery: The Negro in the Free States, 1790-1860* (Chicago, 1961). Eugene H. Berwanger, *The Frontier Against Slavery* (Urbana, 1967).

[61] *Cincinnati Journal,* January 26, February 2, 1830; June 6, 1834; June 14, 1838. *Northwestern Advocate,* March 16, 1853. *Western Advocate,* December 4, 1835; November 28, 1860. *Christian Times,* October 20, 1853. *Michigan Christian Herald,* February 19, 1852. *Cross and Journal,* November 27, 1846.

[62] *Michigan Christian Herald,* February 19, 1852; June 23, 1853.

[63] *Cross and Journal,* November 27, 1846.

[64] *Watchman of the Valley,* July 1, 1847.
[65] *Cincinnati Journal,* October 5, 1832; January 13, 1832.
[66] *Western Advocate,* November 7, 1845; February 23, 1853. *Watchman of the Valley,* July 1, 1847. *Journal and Messenger,* January 23, 1852.
[67] *Northwestern Advocate,* March 2, 1853. *Western Advocate,* February 25, 1848. *Christian Times,* August 31, 1853.
[68] *Watchman of the Valley,* January 21, 1847. *Oberlin Evangelist,* February 13, 1839; March 15, 1843.

BIBLIOGRAPHY OF RELIGIOUS NEWSPAPERS WITH LIBRARY HOLDINGS

The most important source in compiling a complete list and reliable description of religious newspapers is the medium itself. Editors exchanged papers with each other and carefully followed the development of the religious press in their own and other denominations. There are several contemporary lists derived from census returns or denominational records which give most of the newspapers for the year or years involved but with a minimum of descriptive material. Orville A. Roorbach, *Bibliotheca Americana* ... (New York, 1852) and Joseph C. G. Kennedy, "Catalogue of the Newspapers and Periodicals Published in the United States ... ," *Livingston's Law Register for 1852* (New York, 1852) are relatively complete for the census year. The latter gives circulation figures for many of the papers in 1850. Daniel J. Kenny, *The American Newspaper Directory: Lists and Records of the Press of the United States* (New York, 1861) and William Turner Coggeshall, *The Newspaper Record*, ... (Philadelphia, 1856) are similar sources. Joseph Belcher, *The Religious Denominations of the United States* ... (Philadelphia, 1857) and Alexander David Schem, *The American Ecclesiastical Yearbook* ... (New York, 1860) are examples of compilations of denominational activities and statistics including periodicals.

The most useful tool in locating files is the *Union List of Serials* ... , revised edition (1965), although even the revision is not reliable for library holdings in many cases. Gordon Albaugh, "American Presbyterian Periodicals and Newspapers, 1752-1830, With Library Locations," a series of four articles in the *Journal of Presbyterian History*, XLI-XLII (September, 1963—June, 1964) is complete for the period and even contains some information beyond 1830. The series by Eugene P. Willging and Herta Hatzfeld, *Catholic Serials of the Nineteenth Century in the United States: A Descriptive Bibliography and Union List* (Washington, D. C.) which includes volumes for Wisconsin (1960), Illinois (1961), Indiana (1962), Michigan (1964), and Ohio combined with Kentucky (1966) incorporates and supersedes all previous bibliography relating to Catholic journalism. The *Union List of Baptist Serials* (Fort Worth,

1960) and Claude E. Spencer, *Periodicals of the Disciples of Christ and Related Religious Groups* (Canton, Missouri, 1943) rely upon other union lists, hence are not as complete or as accurate as the former. I. S. Bradley, "Bibliography of Available Documentary and Newspaper Material for the Old Northwest," *American Historical Association Report,* I (1896), 296-319 lists many religious newspapers.

There are several published catalogues for major collections and areas in the Old Northwest. *Newspapers in Libraries of Metropolitan Chicago* (Chicago, 1931) has a section on religious newspapers. Others are: C. B. Galbreath, *Newspapers and Periodicals in the Ohio State Library* (Columbus, 1902); Ada Tyng Griswold, *Annotated Catalogue of Newspaper Files in the Library of the State Historical Society of Wisconsin* (Madison, 1911); Arthur D. Mink, *Union List of Ohio Newspapers Available in Ohio* (Columbus, 1946); and "Newspapers in the Illinois State Historical Library," *Illinois Libraries,* XXXVIII, 6, Supplement (June, 1955). Franklin W. Scott, *Newspapers and Periodicals in Illinois, 1814-1879* (Springfield, 1910) is complete and contains a minimum of error. Another statewide survey is Fava E. Goan, *Union List of Serials in Indiana Libraries* (Lafayette, 1940). Collections of religious newspapers have expanded very little since even the earlier compilations except for microfilm reproductions in a few cases.

The main titles used in the newspaper list are those by which papers were most commonly known. Other titles are given with cross references. Circulation figures are given by numeral and the year for which the figure was revealed. The ultimate source of any circulation figures is the paper itself. The symbols used to indicate library holdings conform to usage in the *Union List*. The holdings are those confirmed by the author and in terms that reveal the proportion of the original issues in a file, except that individual issues may be given when holdings are scattered. No terminal date means the paper is current or that it continued into the twentieth century.

AGITATOR (Cleveland). 1860. Spiritualist weekly. Reference in Alexander D. Schem, *American Ecclesiastical Yearbook* (New York, 1860), 85.

ALTON OBSERVER. Sept. 8, 1836—Aug. 17, 1837. Presbyterian weekly. 2,000 in 1837. ICHi, lacking 2 issues. IHi, lacking 5 issues.

AMERICAN CHRISTIAN REVIEW (Cincinnati). Jan. 5, 1858—Aug. 2, 1883. Disciples weekly. Absorbed *Christian Age*, 1858. 6,000 in 1858. InIC, 1858-1860. File resumes after 1861.

AMERICAN ISRAELITE. *See Israelite.*

ANTI-PAPIST. *See Cincinnati Protestant.*

AURORA (Detroit). Sept. 27, 1851—Dec. 1852. German Catholic weekly. Reference in Willging and Hatzfeld, *Catholic Serials*, Michigan, 15.

BAPTIST BANNER AND PIONEER. A weekly in Louisville, but published simultaneously in New Albany, Indiana, during 1839.

BAPTIST HELMET (Vandalia, Illinois), Nov. 8, 1844—late 1845. Weekly. ICHi, about 60% complete. IHi, Apr. 10, July 9, 1845.

BAPTIST WEEKLY JOURNAL OF THE MISSISSIPPI VALLEY. *See Journal and Messenger.*

BETTER COVENANT (Rockford; St. Charles; Chicago). Jan. 6, 1842—1847. Universalist weekly. Sold to *Star in the West*. ICHi, Jan. 5, 1843—Dec. 18, 1845.

CATHOLIC TELEGRAPH (Cincinnati). Oct. 22, 1831—. Weekly. Absorbed *Catholic Advocate* of Louisville in 1849. Became the *Catholic Telegraph and Advocate* after 1849. 850 in 1837; 1267 in 1841; 8,000 in 1850. DCU, complete except for 1838 and Jan. to July, 1851. InNu, 1831-1832, 1834-1835, 1839-1840, 1855-1860.

CATHOLIC VINDICATOR (Detroit). Apr. 30, 1853—Apr. 25, 1857. Weekly. Became the *Detroit Vindicator* and essentially secular in 1857. MiD-B. MiDU. Mi.

CENTRAL CHRISTIAN HERALD (Cincinnati). June 4, 1840-1869. New School Presbyterian weekly. Began as *Cincinnati Observer; Watchman of the Valley,* Mar. 4, 1841—

161

Mar. 22, 1849; *Central Watchman* until it absorbed the *Indiana Christian Herald*, Nov. 2, 1849 and became *Central Christian Herald; Christian Herald* after 1860 until merger with *Presbyter* in 1869. 1,400 in 1841; 3,200 in 1854; 4,000 in 1861. PPPrHi, nearly complete. TxBL, microfilm of above file. ICMcC, nearly complete. OCIWHi, v. I, 1840-1841 nearly complete; Oct. 1845—Sept. 1846; 1845-1852 scattered issues; 1853-1854 50% complete; 1855-1860 nearly complete. OCHP, 6 widely scattered issues.

CENTRAL WATCHMAN. *See Central Christian Herald.*

CHICAGO EVANGELIST. April 8, 1853-1855. Presbyterian weekly. Absorbed monthly *Alton Reporter* in 1855. More than 1,000. ICHi, one issue which could not be found. Reference in *Northwestern Advocate* Aug. 23, 1854.

CHICAGO RECORD. *See Church Record.*

CHRISTIAN AGE (Cincinnati, except 1850-1852 at Hygeia). 1845-1858. Disciples weekly. Absorbed monthly *Protestant Unionist* in 1848 and the *Sower* in 1855, adapting title accordingly. Merged with *American Christian Review*. About 4,000 at peak; 2,000 in 1858. MWA, Dec. 2, 1852. OCIWHi, ten issues scattered 1852-1853. NRAB, seven issues 1849, nearly complete Feb. 1850—Jan. 1856. InIC, Jan. 1849—Nov. 1850. OCHP, Mar. 20, 1851.

CHRISTIAN BANKER (Chicago). Jan. 8, 1853—(?) eight issues. Spiritualist weekly. ICHi, Jan. 5, 12, 1853.

CHRISTIAN ERA (Chicago). Aug. 1851(?)—1852 Presbyterian. ICHi, Sept. 4, 1851; Feb. 28, 1852.

CHRISTIAN HERALD (Vevay, Indiana). 1824. Nonsectarian. Reference in Donald F. Carmony, "The Pioneer Press in Indiana," *Indiana History Bulletin,* XXXI (October, 1954), 202-203.

CHRISTIAN HERALD. *See Central Christian Herald.*

CHRISTIAN LEADER (Cincinnati). Oct. or Nov. 1857-1858. Free Presbyterian weekly. Turned over to the *Presbyterian Witness* of the Associate Presbyterian Church. References in *Presbyterian of the West,* Nov. 26, 1857; *Presbyterian Witness,* Jan. 1, 1859.

CHRISTIAN LUMINARY (Cincinnati). July, 1858—April, 1861. Disciples semimonthly to weekly, then became monthly in April, 1861. OClWHi, 8 scattered issues 1859-1861.

CHRISTIAN MESSENGER (Madison; to Indianapolis in 1846). Sept. 1843—Dec. 11, 1849. Baptist semimonthly, then weekly in 1847. Sold to *Christian Journal* of Cincinnati which then became the *Journal and Messenger.* 2,000 by 1847. InFC, nearly complete. In, Apr. 17, July 10, 1845; Sept. 18, 1849.

CHRISTIAN MONITOR (Knightstown, Indiana). 1834. Methodist. Prospectus in *Western Christian Advocate,* Dec. 19, 1834.

CHRISTIAN POLITICIAN (Cincinnati). 1844(?). Baptist weekly. OCHi, Jan. 7, 1844.

CHRISTIAN PRESS (Cincinnati). 1852-1900(?). Largely Congregational weekly, until it became monthly in 1854. OClWHi, Dec. 24, 1852. PGC, Dec. 10, 1852; Feb. 4, 1853. OC holdings only after it became a monthly.

CHRISTIAN REGISTER OF BAPTIST HISTORY, LITERATURE AND INTELLIGENCE (Zanesville, Ohio). May 2, 1850—1853(?). Baptist semimonthly, becoming weekly in 1853. 1,000 or more. OClWHi, first volume complete. NRAB, May 2, 16, 30, 1850. MWA, July 20, 1853.

CHRISTIAN STATESMAN (Mansfield, Ohio). 1853(?). Wesleyan Methodist weekly. References in *Western Advocate,* Feb. 23, 1853; *Oberlin Evangelist,* Mar. 16, 1853.

CHRISTIAN TEACHER. *See Western Universalist.*

CHRISTIAN TELESCOPE. *See Glad Tidings and Ladies Universalist Magazine.*

CHRISTIAN TIMES (Chicago). Aug. 31, 1853—   . Baptist weekly. Successor to the *Watchman of the Prairies.* Absorbed the *Witness* of Indianapolis and the *Michigan Christian Herald* in 1867 and became briefly the *Christian Times and Witness* before becoming the *Standard.* Absorbed the *Illinois Baptist* in 1858. 4,000 in 1854; 5,000 in 1855; 7,000-8,000 by 1863. ICU, nearly complete. NRAB. TXBL, 1853-1855. KyLS. TNSHi.

CHRISTIAN WITNESS AND WESTERN RESERVE AD-VOCATE (Cuyahoga Falls, Ohio). 1843-1844(?). Methodist. References in *Cross and Journal,* Sept. 1, 1843; *Ohio Observer,* Feb. 22, 1844.

CHRISTLICHE APOLOGETE (Cincinnati). 1839-1941. Methodist weekly. 100 in 1839; 1,700 in 1847; 6,175 in 1855; 9,166 in 1860. OCHP, 13 issues in late 1849; 1850-1861. IEG, June 25, 1841—June 7, 1844.

CHRISTLICHE BOTSCHAFTER (New Berlin, Pennsylvania, until 1854; Cleveland). Jan., 1836-1946. Evangelical Association semimonthly, becoming a weekly in 1861. 5,500 in 1854; 9,300 in 1862. INE. ODaEHi.

CHURCH RECORD (Chicago). Apr. 1857—Mar. 1862. Episcopal monthly, becoming semimonthly in 1859. Became *Chicago Record* June 1, 1860, and *Northwestern Church* in 1862. ICHi. WHi. IHi, Apr. 1, 1859—Mar. 15, 1860.

CINCINNATI CHRISTIAN JOURNAL. *See Cincinnati Journal.*

CINCINNATI JOURNAL. May 2, 1829-1839. Plan of Union, but increasingly New School Presbyterian weekly. *Cincinnati Pandect* to Sept. 15, 1829; became *Cincinnati Christian Journal,* then absorbed *Indiana Religious Intelligencer* in 1830 and added *Religious Intelligencer* to its title. Known as *Cincinnati Journal* Dec. 31, 1830—Oct. 23, 1835. Absorbed *Western Luminary* and added it to title until Oct. 19, 1837. Reverted to *Cincinnati Journal* until removed to New York in 1839. 3,600 in 1836. PPPrHi, most complete file available but lacks *Pandect.* TxBL, microfilm of above file. OCHP, May 19, 1829; 1830, 60%; Jan. 6, 1832—Dec. 21, 1837. ICMcC, 1832 nearly complete; 1833 second half complete; 1834-1835 nearly complete; 1838 nearly complete. OC1WHi, Apr. 28, 1836-1838 nearly complete. ICHi, 1835-1837. WHi, 1830—July, 1831.

CINCINNATI OBSERVER. *See Central Christian Herald.*

CINCINNATI PANDECT. *See Cincinnati Journal.*

CINCINNATI PROTESTANT. Oct. 3, 1846—Dec. 18, 1847 except suspended Dec. 19, 1846—Jan. 16, 1847. Anti-Catholic weekly. It absorbed the *True Catholic* of Louisville and became the *Cincinnati Protestant and True Catholic.* PPPrHi.

CINCINNATI REMEMBRANCER. Aug. 10, 1822—July 26, 1823. Presbyterian weekly. OCHP, Mar. 1—June 21, 1823.

CITOYEN (Detroit). May 4, 1850—June, 1851, except suspended Nov. 11, 1850 for some weeks. French Catholic weekly. Reference in Willging and Hatzfeld, *Catholic Serials,* Michigan, 16-17.

CLEVELAND JOURNAL. May or June, 1837—Sept. 21, 1837. Presbyterian weekly. Absorbed *Cleveland Messenger* and united with *Cleveland Observer* Sept. 21, 1837. OC1WHi, July 13-27, 1837.

CLEVELAND MESSENGER. 1836(?), Presbyterian semimonthly. Reference in *Methodist Correspondent,* Oct. 8, 1836.

CLEVELAND OBSERVER. *See Ohio Observer.*

CLOUD AND THE BOW (Chicago). July 7, 1858— (?). Semimonthly. ICHi, July 21, 1858. MWA, July 7, 1858.

CONGREGATIONAL HERALD (Chicago). Apr. 7, 1853— 1861. Weekly, 2,500 in 1855. ICTS, except v.III and v.IV, 1855-1857, which could not be located. IHi, Apr. 11, 1861. MWA, scattered issues but about 50% complete for Mar. 27, 1856—Mar. 19, 1857. TxU, June 19, 1856.

CROSS AND BAPTIST JOURNAL OF THE MISSISSIPPI VALLEY. *See Journal and Messenger.*

DAY STAR. *See Western Midnight Cry.*

DEBORAH (Cincinnati). Aug. 24, 1855—1899. German-Jewish weekly. OCH, except Aug. 21, 1857-1859.

DELAWARE GAZETTE AND RELIGIOUS INFORMER (Delaware, Ohio). Oct. 1, 1818-1819. Nonsectarian weekly. MWA, July 22, 1819.

DETROIT VINDICATOR. *See Catholic Vindicator.*

DAUTSCHE TELESCOPE. *See Froehliche Botschafter.*

EXPOUNDER OF PRIMITIVE CHRISTIANITY. *See Primitive Expounder.*

EVANGELICAL LUTHERAN (Springfield, Ohio). June 16, 1853—Mar. 21, 1856. Lutheran weekly. Sold to *Lutheran Observer.* 1650 by 1856. Reference in Willard D. Allbeck, *A Century of Lutherans in Ohio* (Yellow Springs, 1966), 167.

EVANGELICAL MESSENGER (New Berlin, Pennsylvania to 1854; Cleveland). Jan. 1848-1946. Evangelical Association semimonthly, becoming weekly in 1861. 3,000 in 1855; 4,200 in 1860. INE. ODaEHi. OHi, 1852-1857.

EVANGELICAL OBSERVER (Detroit). Jan.(?), 1845—Oct. 5, 1846(?). Plan of Union, but essentially Presbyterian semimonthly. MiD-B, 5 scattered issues for 1845.

EVANGELICAL UNION (Mt. Pleasant, Ohio). 1845(?). Quaker semimonthly. Reference in *Western Advocate*, March 21, 1845.

EVANGELIST (Tiffin, Ohio). 1857-1864(?). German Reformed weekly. Moved to Cleveland in 1860, eventually merging with *Reformirte Kirkenzeitung*. 1200.

EVANGELISTEN (Galesburg, Illinois). 1859-1861. Swedish Baptist semimonthly. Apparently began as *Frihetsvännen* [Friend of Liberty]. Reference in Adolf Olson, *A Centenary History as Related to the Baptist General Conference of America* (Chicago, 1952), 169.

FAMILY FAVORITE AND TEMPERANCE JOURNAL (Adrian, Michigan), 1849. Methodist weekly then monthly. MiD-B monthly only, Dec. 1849—Sept. 1850.

FREDERICK VISITOR (Frederick [City], Ohio). 1838(?). Probably Methodist weekly. Reference in *Western Advocate*, Sept. 21, 1838.

FREE NATION (Cincinnati). 1861(?). Nonsectarian weekly. References in *Christian Herald*, Jan. 10, Mar. 7, 1861.

FREE PRESBYTERIAN (Mercer, Pennsylvania, 1850-1853; Athens, Ohio, 1853; Yellow Springs, 1854). 1850-1857. Free Presbyterian weekly. Succeeded by the *Christian Leader*. OC1WHi, Aug. 10, 1853—Oct. 1855.

FRIHETSVÄNNEN. *See Evangelisten.*

FROEHLICHE BOTSCHAFTER [*Joyful Messenger*]. (Circleville, Ohio, 1846-1858; Lebanon, Pennsylvania, Oct. 1, 1846—United Brethren semimonthly, except weekly Jan. 4, 1856-1858. Established as the *Deutsche Telescope. Geschaeftige* [*Busy*] *Martha* Nov. 15, 1849—Nov. 11, 1851. 1,158 in 1853; 1,838 in 1857; 960 in 1861. ODaEHi.

GAMBIER OBSERVER or GAMBIER OBSERVER AND WESTERN CHURCH JOURNAL. *See Western Episcopalian.*

GENIUS OF TRUTH (Zanesville, Ohio). 1843. Universalist semimonthly. Absorbed by *Star in the West,* Aug. 5, 1843.

GESCHAEFTIGE MARTHA. *See Froehliche Botschafter.*

GLAD TIDINGS AND LADIES UNIVERSALIST MAGAZINE (Columbus, Ohio, 1836; Pittsburgh, Pennsylvania and Columbus, 1837-1838; Pittsburgh and Akron, Ohio 1838-1839; Akron, 1839-1840). July, 1836-1840. Frequency varied. Founded as monthly *Christian Telescope* in Columbus. United with a Pittsburgh paper in April, 1837 and published as *Glad Tidings and Ohio Christian Telescope* until August, when it became the *Glad Tidings and Ohio Universalist.* Absorbed by the *Star in the West.* 1,100 in 1837. OCHP, nearly complete Aug., 1837—Nov., 1840. OOxM final volume, 1839-1840 nearly complete. OC1WHi, 4 issues 1836-1837.

GOSPEL ADVOCATE. *See Universalist Advocate.*

GOSPEL HERALD (New Carlisle, Ohio, 1843-1845. Springfield, 1845-1854; 1855-1856. Yellow Springs, 1854-1855. Columbus, 1856-1865). 1843-1868. Christian Denomination semimonthly becoming weekly in 1853. Consolidated with the *Herald of Gospel Liberty* in New England. 2,800 in 1844; 3,600 in 1850. OC1WHi, 4 vols., 1843-1848 listed in catalogue but could not be located. InIC, 1 vol., 1846-1847.

GOSPEL HERALD (Voree, Wisconsin). Jan. 1846—June 6, 1850. Mormon monthly, becoming weekly after first volume. First volume was *Voree Herald,* then *Zion's Reveille* until Sept. 23, 1847. WHi, 26 scattered issues. MiD-B microfilm of above file.

GOSPEL HERALD. Universalist. *See Herald and Era.*

GOSPEL LABORER AND BEACON LIGHT (Cincinnati). May 21, 1858—(?). Baptist semimonthly or weekly. OClWHi, May 21, Oct. 8, 1858.

HEMLANDET (Galesburg to 1858; Chicago). 1855-1869. Swedish Lutheran beginning as the semimonthly *Hemlandet, Det Gamla och det Nya* [*Homeland, the Old and the New*].

Det Ratta Hemlandet [*The True Homeland*] was published as a distinctly religious paper to alternate with the former. Merged with *Augustana* in 1869. 800 in 1855. IRA. IHi, 1857-1858. TxU, Jan. 7, 1859—Dec. 27, 1865.

HERALD AND ERA (Madison, Indiana, 1850-1851; Madison and Louisville, 1851-1855; Indianapolis and St. Louis, 1855 with Indianapolis as main center). 1850-1865. Universalist semimonthly becoming weekly in 1853 with semimonthly also issued in 1859. Began as *Gospel Herald* and absorbed monthly *Golden Era* in 1855. Claimed 6,000-7,000 in 1855. In scattered issues otherwise, but 1851-1852, 50% complete; 1855, 75% complete; 1856, 80% complete.

HERALD OF THE PRAIRIES. *See Prairie Herald.*

HERALD OF TRUTH (Cincinnati). Mar. 17, 1825—May 18, 1826. Swedenborgian semimonthly. OCHP, lacks one issue.

HERALD OF TRUTH (Terre Haute, 1847-1848; Madison, 1848-1849). 1846-1849. Universalist monthly becoming semimonthly in 1848. Merged with *Western Universalist.*

ILLINOIS ADVOCATE AND LEBANON JOURNAL. Dec. 1847—Nov. 1852. Methodist semimonthly, becoming weekly in its last volume. Began as *Lebanon Journal* and was *Illinois Christian Advocate* by 1850. Assets taken over by *Central Christian Advocate* of St. Louis. 1,500 in 1850. References in *Western Advocate,* Jan. 7, Nov. 1, 1848; Nov. 28, 1849; Oct. 2, 1850. IHi, Feb. 12, 1852.

INVESTIGATOR (Mishawauka, Indiana). 1846-1847. Disciples semimonthly. Reference in *Primitive Expounder,* May 21, 1846.

ISRAELITE (Cincinnati), July 4, 1854—(?). Reformed Jewish weekly. 2,000 in 1855. OCH.

JOURNAL AND MESSENGER (Cincinnati to 1838; Columbus, 1838-1850 then back to Cincinnati). July 22, 1831—Mar. 18, 1920. Baptist weekly. Began as *Baptist Weekly Journal of the Mississippi Valley.* In 1834 became *Cross and Baptist Journal* . . . having absorbed the *Cross* of Kentucky; 1838, *Cross and Journal;* 1847, *Western Christian Journal;* 1850, *Journal and Messenger.* 560 in 1831; 2,000 in 1836; 1,500 in 1844; 3,000 in 1850. OGraD, 1831-1847. InFC, 1855-1858. NRAB, substantial file through 1847; about 50% complete 1858-1871.

JOURNAL DE L'ILLINOIS (Kankakee, except Sept. 18, 1857—July 16, 1858 in Chicago). Jan. 2, 1857—1863. French Catholic weekly. WHi, Jan. 8—July 2, 1858; Aug. 13-27, 1858. MWA, May 1, 1857.

KATHOLISCHES WOCHENBLATT [*Catholic Weekly*] (Chicago). 1859-1930. German Catholic weekly.

KIRKE TIDENDE FOR DEN SKANDINAVISK EVAN-GELISK-LUTHERSKE KIRKE [*Church Journal....*] (Racine, Wisconsin to Aug. 19, 1853; Norway, Illinois). 1851-1854(?). Norwegian Lutheran semimonthly. 500. IaDL, more than 75% complete Dec. 30, 1851—Sept. 29, 1854.

LEBANON JOURNAL. *See Illinois Advocate and Lebanon Journal.*

LICHT-FREUND [*Friend of Light*] (Cincinnati). 1840-1841(?). Universalist semimonthly. 500. Reference in *Western Advocate,* Feb. 26, 1841.

LUTHERAN STANDARD (Columbus and Marysville, Ohio, after 1847, otherwise moved with pastors to New Philadelphia, Zanesville, Somerset). Sept. 21, 1842—(?). Lutheran weekly, becoming semimonthly in 1846. 950 in 1843; 1,400 in 1856. OCoCU. MoStLC.

LUTHERISCHE KIRCHENZEITUNG [*Church Times*] (Columbus). Jan. 1, 1860—(?). German Lutheran semimonthly. OOxM, 1862-1865.

MEDIUM (Jackson, 1848; to Marshall, then Detroit, 1850). Dec. 25, 1848—1853(?). Swedenborgian semimonthly.

METHODIST CORRESPONDENT (Cincinnati, 1830-1832; Pittsburgh, 1832-1833; Zanesville, 1833-1836). Sept. 1830—Nov. 1836. Methodist Protestant semimonthly. 1,400 in 1835. OOxM, Nov. 22, 1834—Nov. 5, 1836. OHi, Apr. 6, 1833.

METHODIST EXPOSITOR AND TRUE ISSUE (Cincinnati). 1848-1850. Methodist Episcopal Church, South weekly. References in *Western Advocate,* July 12, 1848; *Religious Telescope,* Mar. 6, 1850.

MICHIGAN CHRISTIAN ADVOCATE (Adrian). 1851-1852. Methodist weekly. Prospectus in *Family Favorite,* Jan. 1850.

MICHIGAN CHRISTIAN HERALD (Detroit). Jan. 1842—Dec. 1867. Baptist weekly except monthly, 1842; semimonthly 1843-1844, 1847. Disposed of to *Christian Times*. 1,524 in 1843; 3,000 during 1850's. MiD-B, most volumes complete or nearly so. NRAB, scattered except 1848-1852 complete.

MICHIGAN ESSAY: OR, THE IMPARTIAL OBSERVER (Detroit). Aug. 31, 1809 and perhaps two more issues. Catholic weekly. MiD-B. TxU. ICHi.

MICHIGAN OBSERVER (Detroit). June 17, 1837—June 22, 1839. Presbyterian. References in *Ohio Observer*, Dec. 22, 1836; July 24, 1839.

MINNESOTA POSTEN (Red Wing). 1857-1858. Swedish Lutheran. Both paper and staff absorbed by *Hemlandet*. Reference in Ander, *Hasselquist*, 240.

MISCELLANEOUS REPOSITORY (Mt. Pleasant, Ohio). Feb. 1827—Aug. 16, 1836. Quaker, frequency irregular. InRE. OCHP, Feb. 1827, 1832. WHi, July 2, 1829—July 10, 1830; scattered Sept. 17, 1831—Apr. 6, 1833. OC1WHi, Jan. 1, 1829—Apr. 6, 1833.

NEW CHURCH HERALD (Philadelphia; to Columbus then to Cincinnati in 1858). Oct. 1855—Dec. 1859. Swedenborgian weekly. WHi.

NEW CHURCH MESSENGER (Cincinnati). 1860-1861(?). Swedenborgian semimonthly. OC1WHi, May 18, 1861.

NEW COVENANT (Chicago). Nov. 5, 1848—Sept. 23, 1880. Universalist weekly. Sold to *Star in the West* which moved to Chicago and became *Star and Covenant*. ICHi, very scattered issues, 1851-1859. WHi, May 22, 1852. MWA, May 22, 1858; Jan. 22, July 30, Aug. 20, 1859.

NORSK LUTHERSK KIRKETIDENDE FOR DEN EVANGELISK LUTHERSKE KIRKE I AMERICA [*Norwegian Lutheran Church Times....*] (Leland, Illinois to 1859; Milwaukee). Dec. 4, 1857—Nov. 30, 1860. Semimonthly. IaDL, Dec. 4, 1857—Dec. 14, 1855, nearly complete; Feb. 22, Mar. 22, May 10-17, Dec. 21, 1859—Feb. 1, 1860; Mar. 7—Nov. 3, 1860.

NORTHWESTERN BAPTIST (Chicago). Sept. 20, 1842—Sept. 20, 1844. Semimonthly. Absorbed by *Western Christian*. IHi, 6 widely scattered issues. NRAB, missing only five scattered issues.

NORTHWESTERN CHRISTIAN ADVOCATE (Chicago). Jan. 5, 1853-1939. Methodist weekly. 8,000 in 1854; 13,300 in 1860. IEG.

NORTHWESTERN CHURCH. *See Church Record.*

NORTHWESTERN INTELLIGENCER (Galesburg, Illinois) 1848-1850. Presbyterian weekly. IU, Dec. 7, 1849.

OBERLIN EVANGELIST. Nov. 1, 1838—Dec. 17, 1862. Independent Congregationalist semimonthly. 5,000 in 1839; 4,300 in 1850; 2,500 in late 1850's. OO. OC1WHi. WHi. TxDaM, 1838-1847, 1851-1852, 1856-1862. OCHP, 1840-1845. IEG, 1838-1848, 1852, 1855-1862 about 50% complete. InU, 1839, 1843. 1845-1847, 1850.

OBSERVER AND TELEGRAPH. *See Ohio Observer.*

OHIO OBSERVER (Cleveland, 1827-1828, 1837-1840; Hudson, 1828-1837, 1840-1855). July 20, 1827—June 20, 1855. Plan of Union weekly but largely Presbyterian. Began as *Western Intelligencer; Observer and Telegraph,* 1830-1833; *Ohio Observer,* 1833-1837, 1840-1855; *Cleveland Observer,* 1837-1840. Absorbed *Cleveland Journal* and *Cleveland Observer* in 1837. Absorbed *Independent Register* and *Family Visitor* in Cleveland in 1854 and issued *Visitor* as a secular section. Sold to *New York Evangelist.* 1,200 in 1830; 1,050 in 1850. OC1WHi, TxBL, microfilm of above file.

OHIO UNIVERSALIST AND LITERARY COMPANION (Cleveland). 1845-1846. Weekly. Merged with *Western Evangelist* at Buffalo. OC1WHi, 4 issues listed but could not be located.

OLIVE BRANCH (Springfield, Illinois). 1856-1860. Lutheran monthly but projected as semimonthly in 1857. References in *Lutheran Standard,* Feb. 3, 1857; Ander, *Hasselquist,* 45.

OLIVE BRANCH OF THE WEST (Chicago). Sept. 9, 1853—1854. Baptist weekly but irregular. ICHi, Oct. 1853—Jan. 19, 1854, 4 issues missing.

OLIVE LEAF (Vandalia, Illinois). 1844(?)-1845. Methodist Protestant weekly. References in *Western Recorder,* Dec. 5, 1844; June 19, 1845. IHi, Jan. 29, 1845.

PHILANTHROPIST (Mt. Pleasant, Ohio). Sept. 12, 1817—May 15, 1822. Quaker weekly. OHi. Second series, OC1WHi, complete except for a few issues 1820-1821.

InRE, complete except has only Jan. 29, 1820 in v.III, 1819-1820. OHi, a few scattered issues.

PIONEER OF THE VALLEY OF THE MISSISSIPPI (Rock Springs, Illinois to 1836; Alton). Apr. 25, 1829—Dec. 13, 1838. Baptist semimonthly, until it became weekly in 1836. *Pioneer and Western Baptist* briefly in 1830; known as *Western Pioneer* then *Pioneer* in 1835 and *Western Pioneer* again after 1835; became *Western Pioneer and Baptist Standard Bearer* in Alton. Absorbed into the *Baptist Banner and Western Pioneer* of Louisville. ICHi, Sept. 1, 1830; July 17, 1835; June 30, 1836—Dec. 13, 1838, about 60% complete. MWA, July 10, 1829.

PORT WASHINGTON ZEITUNG (Wisconsin). Jan. 1, 1855-1928. German Catholic weekly. WHi, Aug. 25, 1859, listed but not located.

PRAIRIE HERALD (Chicago). Apr. 1, 1846-1853. Plan of Union weekly. Began as *Western Herald; Herald of the Prairies*, 1848-1849. Successors were the *Chicago Evangelist, Presbyterian,* and the *Congregational Herald,* resulting from a breakdown in the Plan of Union. 3,000 in 1849. ICMcC, Apr. 1, 1846—Aug. 1, 1849 except Apr. 7, 1847—Nov. 27, 1848, could not be located; Apr. 1, 1851—Mar. 23, 1852. IHi, July 21, 1847—Feb. 18, 1851.

PRESBYTER. *See Central Christian Herald* and *Presbyterian of the West.*

PRESBYTERIAN OF THE WEST (Springfield to 1845; Cincinnati). Sept. 22, 1841—Sept. 22, 1869. Old School Presbyterian semimonthly becoming weekly in 1845. Changed to *Presbyter* in 1859. 2,800 in 1850. PPPrHi, complete except late 1845—late 1848. OC1WHi, 5 scattered issues 1841-1845; nearly complete 1847-1849. TxU, 1855-1858. In, 30% complete 1850-1856. ICMcC, complete after Jan. 6, 1859. No file as listed at OC1WHi.

PRESBYTERIAN EXPOSITOR (Chicago). 1857—May, 1861. Old School Presbyterian monthly, becoming weekly in 1860. References in *Presbytery Reporter*, Feb., 1860; *Congregational Herald,* Jan. 12, 1860.

PRESBYTERIAN WITNESS (Cincinnati). Feb. 1853-1868. Associate Presbyterian semimonthly, becoming weekly in

1859. Absorbed the *Christian Leader* in 1859. PPPrHi, about 50% complete, 1853-1856; 65% complete, 1857; nearly complete, 1859-1861.

PRIMITIVE EXPOUNDER (Ann Arbor 1843-1844, 1847-1848; Alphadelphia, 1844-1846; Jackson, 1846-1847; Lansing, 1848-1852). 1843-1852. Universalist semimonthly. Known briefly as *Expounder of Primitive Christianity*. Sold to *Star in the West*. 1,920 in 1848. MiD-B, nearly complete except for first volume. Mi, few scattered issues, 1843-1852. WHi.

PROGRESSIVE FRIEND (Elgin, Illinois). 1860. Spiritualist weekly. Reference in Schem, *Ecclesiastical Yearbook*, 85.

PROTESTANT MONITOR (Greenville, Illinois; briefly in Alton, 1848). Dec. 1845-1848. Methodist Protestant weekly. IHi, Dec. 8, 1845—Dec. 25, 1846 nearly complete; Jan. 22—Dec. 8, 1847, about 25% complete; Jan. 19—May 24, 1848, about 50% complete. ICHi, Dec. 17, 1845; Mar. 5, Aug. 18, 1847.

RELIGIOUS TELESCOPE (Circleville to 1853; Dayton). Dec. 1834-1946. United Brethren semimonthly, becoming weekly in 1845. 1,502 in 1842; 5,000 in 1850; 11,443 in 1857; 7,800 in 1861. ODaEHi. TxBL, July 1845-1861.

RETINA (Cincinnati). July 1, 1843—July 5, 1844. Swedenborgian weekly. WHi. OHi, six issues.

SÄNDEBUDET (Rockford, Illinois to 1864; Chicago). July 18, 1862-   . Swedish Methodist semimonthly. Reference in Ander, *Hasselquist*, 243.

SEEBOTE [*Messenger of the Lake*] (Milwaukee). Dec., 1851-1870. Catholic weekly with secular daily edition beginning 1852. WMSF, Feb. 1, 1854—Jan. 29, 1855; Jan. 30, 1856—Dec. 26, 1860. Only holdings listed for religious phase of paper.

SENTINEL AND STAR IN THE WEST. See *Star in the West*.

SPIRITUAL MESSENGER (Cincinnati). 1856. Spiritualist, semimonthly. OCHP, May 3, 1856.

SPIRITUAL UNIVERSE (Cleveland). 1854-1855. Spiritualist, published irregularly. OC1WHi, Mar. 17, June 16, 1855.

STANDARD (Cincinnati to 1834; South Hanover, Indiana). Sept. 7, 1831—Dec. 31, 1835. Old School Presbyterian weekly. Became the *Western Presbyterian* in 1836 which was sold to Joseph Monfort who began the *Western Presbyterian Herald* in Louisville. PPPrHi. OC1WHi, 1831-1834 nearly complete; five issues of *Western Presbyterian* in card catalogue but could not be located. OHi, 65% complete, Sept. 7, 1831—Oct. 4, 1833. InU, 1831-1834, scattered.

STAR IN THE WEST (Eaton, Ohio, 1827-1829; Cincinnati, 1829-1833, 1836-1880; Philomath, Indiana, 1833-1836). Aug., 1827-1880. Universalist monthly, becoming weekly in 1829. *Sentinel and Star in the West,* 1829-1838; again *Star in the West* until 1840, when it absorbed *Glad Tidings* and appended it to title; beginning 1845 original title resumed until *Star* merged with the *New Covenant* to form the *Star and Covenant* in Chicago. 1,000 in 1835; 2,300 in 1840; about 8,000 in 1854. In, Oct. 23, 1830—Nov. 12, 1831; July 20, 1832—Nov. 11, 1837; July, 1842—Oct., 1845, nearly complete; scattered issues, 1848-1856; 75% complete 1857-1861. OCHP, Oct. 23, 1830—Oct. 22, 1831; Apr., 1840—Apr. 1842; Apr. 15, 1843—Apr. 5, 1845; a few scattered issues otherwise. OC, Oct. 30, 1830—Oct. 22, 1831; Nov. 19, 1831—Feb. 15, 1834; Apr. 27, 1844—Apr. 4, 1846. OCHi, Oct. 3, 1829—Oct. 16, 1830; Nov. 19, 1831—Nov. 10, 1832; Sept. 25, 1841—Apr. 18, 1844; a few other widely scattered issues. OC1WHi, about sixty widely scattered issues Nov. 1847—Dec., 1853. WHi, Oct. 3, 1829—Oct. 22, 1830; Aug. 6, 1836—Aug. 26, 1837; Apr. 2, 1853—Mar. 21, 1857.

STAR AND COVENANT or STAR IN THE WEST AND GLAD TIDINGS. *See Star in the West.*

TIMES AND SEASONS (Nauvoo, Illinois). Nov. (?), 1839—Feb. 15 , 1846. Mormon monthly, then semimonthly. ICHi, 75% complete. InU, Nov., 1840—Feb. 1846. IEG.

UNITED PRESBYTERIAN OF THE WEST (Monmouth, Illinois). Jan. 7, 1857—July, 1861. Associate Reformed weekly. Name changed to *Western United Presbyterian* during last year. Sold to *Christian Instructor* of Philadelphia. PPPrHi, complete except last few issues.

UNIVERSALIST ADVOCATE (Centreburg, Ohio). Sept. 26, 1848-1852(?). Semimonthly. Apparently became *Gospel Advocate* in 1851.

VOREE HERALD. *See Gospel Herald.*

WAHRHEITSFREUND [*Friend of Truth*] (Cincinnati). July 20, 1837-1910. Catholic weekly, daily edition attempted in 1847. IU, July 30, 1837—Aug. 31, 1843; Sept. 5, 1844—Aug. 28, 1845; Sept. 9, 1847—Aug. 31, 1848; Aug. 31, 1854—Aug. 12, 1863.

WATCHMAN OF THE PRAIRIES (Chicago). Aug. 10, 1847—Feb. 22, 1853. Baptist weekly. Sold to group who founded *Christian Times.* 2,000 in 1851. ICU, nearly complete. ICHi. NRAB. LNB. TxFS. TNSHi. KyLS.

WATCHMAN OF THE VALLEY. *See Central Christian Herald.*

WEEKLY RECORDER (Chillicothe, Ohio). July 5, 1814—Oct. 6, 1821. Presbyterian weekly. OCHP. PPPrHi. OHi. OOxM, complete except for v.I. ICU, July 31, 1816—Oct. 6, 1821. OC1WHi, July 11, 1815—July 24, 1816, Aug. 18, 1819—Oct. 6, 1821, and scattered issues otherwise. MWA, nearly complete July 31, 1816—Aug. 17, 1820. WHi, July 5, 1814—July 31, 1818; remainder 50% complete.

WESLEYAN OF THE WEST (Cincinnati). Sept. 21, 1844-(?). Wesleyan Methodist weekly. Reference in *Western Recorder*, Oct. 31, 1844. OC1WHi, Sept. 21, 1844, but not located.

WESTERN CATHOLIC REGISTER (Detroit). July 16, 1842—Apr. 22, 1843. Weekly. 100 or more in 1842. 300 in 1843. MiDDS. MiD-B, July 30, 1842.

WESTERN CHRISTIAN (Elgin, Illinois). Jan. 15, 1845—1849(?). American Baptist Free Mission weekly. Sold to *American Baptist* in New York. 620 in 1845. ICHi, complete June 14—Dec. 31, 1845, and 18 widely scattered issues thereafter.

WESTERN CHRISTIAN ADVOCATE (Cincinnati). May 2, 1834—1939. Methodist weekly. 14,000 in 1840; 18,000 in 1850; 31,000 in 1861. IEG. OC, May 2, 1834—May 12,

1837, nearly complete. OC1WHi, 1857-1860 nearly complete. ODW, nearly complete except v.VIII, 1840-1841. TxBL, 1834-1859. InGD, holdings slight.

WESTERN CHRISTIAN JOURNAL. *See Journal and Messenger.*

WESTERN EPISCOPALIAN (Gambier, Ohio, to 1846, 1848-1858; Mt. Vernon, 1846-1848; Cincinnati, 1858). May 28, 1830—May 25, 1868; not published Oct. 5, 1842—Aug. 11, 1843. Alternately semimonthly and weekly, until it became weekly in 1848. *Gambier Observer* to 1837; *Gambier Observer and Western Church Journal,* 1837-1841; *Western Episcopal Observer,* 1841-1843; *Western Episcopalian,* 1843-1848; *Western Episcopalian and Gambier Observer,* 1848-1855. 1,200 subscribers in 1841; 500 in 1846; 960 in 1855; 1,000 in 1860. OGK, complete except, May 1857—Mar., 1859. OC1WHi, nearly complete 1830-1845; 1853-1855; 1860-1861. OCHP, scattered issues for 1841; nearly complete, July 16, 1858—May 27, 1859.

WESTERN EPISCOPAL OBSERVER. *See Episcopal Observer.*

WESTERN EVANGELIST (Detroit). 1850(?)-1852(?).

WESTERN FOUNTAIN (Greenville, Illinois) Jan., 1849—May(?), 1852. Methodist Protestant semimonthly. 400 in 1850. Reference in *Western Recorder,* Apr. 12, Aug. 9, 1849.

WESTERN FRIEND (Cincinnati). Nov. 11, 1847—Dec. 13, 1849. Quaker weekly. InRE. OCHP, Nov. 11, 1847—Dec. 7, 1848. OHi, Nov. 11, 1847—Dec. 7, 1848. TxU, 1848.

WESTERN HERALD. *See Prairie Herald.*

WESTERN INTELLIGENCER. *See Ohio Observer.*

WESTERN METHODIST PROTESTANT. *See Western Recorder.*

WESTERN MIDNIGHT CRY (Cincinnati to 1846; Union Village). Sept. 20, 1843—July 1, 1847. Adventist and, later, Shaker weekly. Claimed 10,000 copies being distributed, nearly all gratis, in 1844. InU, Dec. 9, 1843—Feb., 1846. OCHP, Dec. 9, 1843—July 1, 1847. WHi, Sept. 27, Dec. 4, 1843—June 29, 1844. OC1WHi, Dec. 27, 1845—July 1, 1847.

WESTERN MISSIONARY (Columbus to 1850; 1853-1856; Tiffin, 1850-1853; Dayton, 1856). Oct. 6, 1848—1867. German Reformed semimonthly. United with *Reformed Church Messenger.* 1,300 in 1849; 2,200 in 1857. PLFM.

WESTERN OBSERVER (Jacksonville, Illinois). May 8, 1830—June 4, 1831. Plan of Union weekly. IaB and IHi, a few issues missing. MWA, Jan. 15, 1830.

WESTERN OLIVE BRANCH. *See Western Universalist.*

WESTERN PIONEER or WESTERN PIONEER AND BAPTIST STANDARD BEARER. *See Pioneer of the Valley of the Mississippi.*

WESTERN PREDESTINARIAN BAPTIST (Paris, Illinois to Oct., 1843; Charleston). Spring, 1842—May 15, 1846. Semimonthly. InFC, Mar. 1, 1842—Dec. 1, 1843.

WESTERN PRESBYTERIAN. *See Standard.*

WESTERN PROTESTANT (Cincinnati). 1845(?). Anti-Catholic semimonthly. Reference in *Watchman of the Valley,* June 5, 1855.

WESTERN RECORDER (Zanesville and nearby Putnam, Ohio to 1855; Springfield). July 18, 1839—1939. Methodist Protestant weekly. Became the *Western Methodist Protestant* in 1855 and *Western Recorder* again in 1866. 2,930 in 1856. InU, July 18, 1839—Oct. 1856. OC1WHi, Mar. 25, 1842. OHi, Aug. 1, 1860.

WESTERN RESERVE CABINET AND FAMILY VISITOR (Ravenna, Ohio). 1840-1843. Nonsectarian weekly. 2,000 in 1843. References in *Oberlin Evangelist,* Jan. 15, 1840; *Ohio Observer,* Mar. 9, 1843. ICHi, Nov. 30, 1841.

WESTERN STAR (Jacksonville, Illinois). Jan. 17, 1845—Dec., 1846. Baptist semimonthly. Sold to *Watchman of the Prairies.* 700 in 1846. ICHi, ten scattered issues. IHi, 1845 nearly complete, 1846, 50% complete. NRAB, nearly complete.

WESTERN TABLET (Chicago). Jan. 31, 1852-1855. Catholic weekly. 2,000 in 1852. ICHi, Jan. 31, 1852—Oct. 29, 1853.

WESTERN UNITED PRESBYTERIAN. *See United Presbyterian of the West.*

WESTERN UNIVERSALIST (Lafayette to 1845; Terre Haute, 1845-1847; Indianapolis, 1847-1849; Cincinnati, 1849). Apr., 1841-1849. Began as monthly becoming semimonthly in 1843. Began as *Christian Teacher* becoming *Western Universalist and Christian Teacher* 1844-1845, after which it was *Western Universalist*. Replaced by *Western Olive Branch*, which was absorbed into the *Star in the West* after a few issues. 800 in 1843. In v.IV, 1844-1845 about 75% complete; v.VI 1846-1847, ten of first twelve issues. OC1WHi, four issues of *Western Olive Branch* listed, but could not be located.

WITNESS (Indianapolis). Sept. 25, 1856-1867. Baptist weekly. Sold to *Christian times* of Chicago. 5,000 in 1859, InFC, Sept. 25, 1856—Dec. 29, 1858.

ZION'S ADVOCATE (Salem, Indiana). Aug., 1829—1831. United Brethren semimonthly. OdaEHi, Oct. 23, Nov. 20, 1830; Jan. 14, 1831.

ZION'S ADVOCATE AND WESLEYAN REGISTER (Cincinnati). Jan. 1—July 30, 1825. Methodist weekly. OCHP, Jan. 1—July 30, 1825, lacking only May 7 and July 4.

ZION'S REVEILLE. *See Gospel Herald* (Voree).

INDEX

Index

controversy with Douglas, 122-123

defends advertising, 21

English immigrant, 27

on importance of editorial, 33

on Know Nothings, 57

office vandalized, 32

on Republican party, 125

temperance advocate, 32

use of exchange material, 34. *See also Northwestern Christian Advocate*

Wealth, 97

Webster-Ashburton Treaty, 106

Webster, Daniel, 88, 106, 119

Weekly Recorder, 175

antislavery views, 112

commodities for subscriptions, 16

founding, 2-3

on Sabbath observance, 76

on temperance, 78

Weld, Theodore Dwight, 111, 112

Wesleyan of the West, 175

Wesleyan Methodists, 112

Western Catholic Register, 175

on temperance, 79

Western Christian, 175

editor's preference for pastorate, 39

Western Christian Advocate, 175-176

assistant editors, 29

circulation, 10

editor demeans United Brethren colleague, 46

editors become bishops, 26

financial success, 10

issue of slavery and change of editors, 43

patent medicine advertising, 21-22

Western Christian Advocate on:

antislavery politics, 119

banking, 99

educational discipline, 103

gag rule, 115-116

public executions, 86

public schools, 102

Western Episcopalean, 176

on Union cause, 129

Western Evangelist, 176

Western Fountain, 176

Western Friend, 176

on Manifest Destiny, 108

Western Herald, antislavery, 118

Western Intelligencer:

grain for subscriptions, 16

warns of Catholic encroachment, 48

Western Mechanic, 96

Western Methodist Protestant: circulation, 10

Western Midnight Cry, 64, 176

Western Missionary, 177

circulation, 12

integrity of advertising, 23

management, 12

Western Observer, 177

Western Predestinarian Baptist, 177

Western Protestant, 177

Western Recorder, 10, 177

on political parties, 120-121

Western Reserve:

development, 3

Mormon colony in, 62

Presbyterian activity, 6

sexual sins in, 82

Western Reserve Cabinet, 177

Western Reserve University, 82

Western Star, 177

Western Tablet, 177

working class interests, 96

Western Universalist, 178

Whig party, 119, 124

White Pigeon, Michigan, 126

Whittier, John Greenleaf, 37